Womens Contribution to India's Economic Resurgence Women Leadership

Womens Contribution to India's Economic Resurgence Women Leadership

Deepali Pant Joshi

GYAN

Womens Contribution to India's Economic Resurgence

Dr Deepali Pant Joshi

Price: ₹ 725
ISBN: 978-81-212-1332-5

First Published, 2016

Gyan Publishing House
5, Ansari Road, Darya Ganj, New Delhi-I10002
Phone: 9811692060
E-mail : books@gyanbooks.com

Cover Image Created Mr Kunal Joshi

Printed at: G. Print Process, Delhi.

Contents

For my father

Shri Jagdish Mohan Pant

(Former Administrator General Official Trustee of the State of Uttar Pradesh)

"whose blessings make all things possible".

"Jo Sab tab Pratap Raghurai,
Nath na Kachhu Mor Prabhutai"

Hanumanji

Extract from the Sundarkand.

This work has been achieved through the benevolence and Grace of the Almighty; to Him alone I attribute the successful achievement of this task.

—Ramayana

Acknowledgements

Most things in my life have been possible due to the blessings and inspiration of my late and beloved father Mr Jagdish Mohan Pant who always believed in me, to him I dedicate this work.

I acknowledge the many debts of gratitude owed to my family, my encouraging mother, Professor Chandra Pant. My husband Rajeev and my affectionate sons Paritosh and Kunal who support and encourage all my endeavours.

The views expressed are my personal views and do not reflect the views of the Reserve Bank of India with which I am associated for a little over three decades.

I extend sincere thanks to Gyan publishing House, the publisher of this work and anticipatory thanks to the prospective readers of the book.

Dr (Smt) Deepali Pant Joshi

Reserve Bank of India

Introduction

A central driver of economic growth over the past two decades in India is the increased role of women in economic life. Since India embraced economic reforms in the early nineties, several positive changes have taken place in the status of women. Gender disparities in women's economic participation reduced significantly. Denying women opportunities to realise their potential is a waste of human capital and bar to economic progress. Due to improved educational attainments, women have joined the workforce in larger numbers. The composition of the labour force has undergone change to accommodate white-collar women workers. New sunrise industries have come up which require specialised skill sets such as software development, pharma industries, where a large number of qualified women engineers find employment. The call centre revolution, the outsourcing of jobs, like medical transcription, tuitions and the online e-retail revolution, enables women to be part of the larger market place and provides them with instant retail distribution channels. This factor among several others led to this upswing in the growth of women's contribution to India's economic resurgence enabling women to move into leadership and managerial roles.The high savings rates which India enjoys 30 per cent of GDP can also be attributed to the thrifty nature of Indian women and their penchant for saving. Women continue to lag far behind men in terms of even literacy, at 34.5 per cent (Census 2011). India's high growth rate – stems from a high rate of saving and capital formation. India achieved a remarkable savings rate of

33 per cent of the GDP, of which 70 per cent comes from household saving and only 20 per cent from the private corporate sector and 10 per cent from public sector undertakings. There are increased savings, consumption attitude and tendency to recycle. Networks of women groups such as NGOs, associations and co-operatives at the grassroots level play a pivotal role in taking initiatives which result in socio-economic development and lead to sustainable scalable income generating activities. In urban India, at the lowest strata, women despite the lack of education and facing problems like shelter, are the architects of social change and economic development by contributing substantial labour force tn various industries like construction of residential & commercial buildings, roads, water bodies, engaging in various domestic and community services etc. While educated women breaching existing stereotypes of teacher, nurse,secretary have emerged as Professors respected academics, Banker's, Board Members Corporate head honchos.

The 2012 World Economic Forums GENDER GAP INDEX REPORT The Gender Gap Index Report ranked India 123rd out of 135 countries on economic participation and opportunity. In 2015 the same report, reflected improvement in India's rank to 108 out of 145 countries. Out of 145 countries, India ranks 139th on the Economic Participation and Opportunity pillar. We still need to create an enabling environment for harnessing the economic potential of the female half of its our population. While exact data on the number of women in skilled and leadership positions, is unavailable India ranks 136th in terms of labour force participation, 139th for estimated earned income and 129th on perceived wage equality for similar work with men. India (108) moved up six positions in the Global Gender Gap Index 2015 compared to 2014 on account of improvements in the Health and Survival and Political Empowerment "pillars". In a year, India has more than doubled the percentage of women in ministerial positions (from 9 per cent to 22 per cent). It now ranks second in the region on the Political Empowerment pillar (it used to rank third last year on that pillar). Another positive element is that India's performance on the Healthy life expectancy indicator slightly improved. Change is slow but it is happening. All relevant actors need to continue to work together to close this gap.

Larger number of employed women, outside the home led to the growth of ancillary industries. Reasonable home-cooked meals delivered to the workplace or the home, crèches and other supportive infrastructure as the improvement in public transport, setting up of working women's hostels also allows women to attain their potential to achieve the full fruition of their persnality. The workforce, begin earning and contributing to the household and also allows women to emerge as consumers of goods and services. This revolution has, in the last decade, led to significant improvement in the status of women and economic development. The bright side of economic growth is dynamic, urban, globally integrated, and rapidly growing. The dark side is rural, poor and not well integrated with the markets. This book concerns itself with the bright side the triumphs and travails of the white and blue collar-working women. Despite considerable progress, women suffer from lack of policy support and severe policy distortions. Acceleration of the reform process, allows Women to achieve their potential to achieve and sustain higher economic growth. The book identifies key drivers of growth and the policies and institutions that have the potential to propel India to higher economic growth while also promoting growth inclusiveness by enhancing skills, and strengthening institutions. It is well accepted, that empowering Women to participate fully in economic life across all sectors throughout all levels of economic activity is an imperative for building strong sustainable economies and just societies, this will also help attain Internationally – agreed goals for development, sustainability and human rights; Improve the quality of life for women, men, families and communities;

MACRO POLICY LEVEL SUPPORT deliberate policies, targeted actions and concrete deliverables are required to harness women's talents, skills, focus on key elements integral to ensuring gender equity in the workplace, marketplace and community.

GENDER LENS Companies have to see their present practices through a gender lens ie from the viewpoint of the women who work for them. Companies need to survey and analyse current practices, benchmarks and reporting practices. Companies need to customise their existing policies and programmes – or establish needed new ones-tailored to helping women. Achieving gender equality is neither simple nor easy and requires the participation of all actors. Each person man or woman should have the inherent ability to realise their full potential. While much can be achieved through integration of principles and actions on corporate responsibility, diversity and inclusion, the full participation of women in the economic life of the nation– from the CEO's office to the factory floor to the supply chain –remains an unfulfilled aspiration to date. Women have the potential to contribute much more to economic resurgence. A gender lens is needed to facilitate the efforts to the attainment of gender equality.

GLOBALISED WORLD AND THE RIGHTS OF WOMEN In 2006 the Economist provocatively proclaimed: "Forget China, India and the internet: Economic growth is driven by women." However, a decade later gender based financial exclusion continues to be deeply ingrained across the world. According to a recent paper by the World Bank[1] more than 1.3 billion women are "largely outside the formal financial system". Regionally, the gap is largest in South Asia, where 41 per cent of men report having a savings account compared to only 25 per cent of women.(Demirguc-Kunt, A., Klapper, L., & Singer, D. (2013) "Financial inclusion and legal discrimination against women: Evidence from developing countries")

Women in South Asia, find it more difficult, to obtain credit, whether from a bank or a more informal moneylender compared to men, as they lack collateral. Gender issues have been playing an integral part of the global development agenda for quite a while. Promoting gender equality and empowering women is one of the Millennium Development Goals.

Gender Diversity Contributes to Success

In an increasingly globalized and interconnected world, utilizing all social and economic assets is crucial for success. Women should not be subject to discrimination, marginalisation and exclusion, even though equality between men and women stands as a universal international precept – a fundamental and inviolable human right. All countries recognise the standards contained in International human rights treaties, which articulate a broad range of civil, political, economic, social and cultural rights. Internationally agreed – on documents such as the Beijing Platform for Action adopted by all 189 countries on Women in 1995 and the Millennium Declaration adopted by 189 countries in 2000, contribute to the overarching human rights framework for women. UN Women, the UN Global Compact, other leading UN agencies, the World Bank and the World Economic Forum, reinforce the finding that gender diversity contributes to the growth of companies. In a globally interdependent economic environment, gender diversity on corporate boards has an increasingly vital role for a vibrant business environment involving a larger spectrum of actors, and allows greater opportunities for women to fulfil their potential; gender diversity on company boards contributes to business excellence.

To encourage women to come to the fore organisations need to articulate clear company-wide goals and targets for gender equality and include progress towards these goals as an important factor in managers' performance and company success Ensure that all policies are gender-sensitive – identifying factors that impact women and men differently – and that corporate culture advances equality and inclusion.

Equal Opportunity, inclusion and Non-discrimination

Ensure that workplace policies and practices are free from gender-based discrimination. Implement gender-sensitive recruitment and retention practices. Proactively recruit and appoint women to managerial and executive positions and to the corporate board of directors. Assure sufficient participation of women in decision-making and governance at all levels and across all business areas. Offer flexible work option, leave and re-entry opportunities to positions of equal pay and status. Support access to child and dependent care by providing services, resources and information to both women and men.

Establish a zero-tolerance policy towards all forms of violence at work, including verbal and/or physical abuse and prevent sexual harassment.

Education and Training

Invest in workplace policies and programmes that open avenues for advancement of women at all levels and across all business areas, and encourage women to enter non-traditional job fields.Ensure equal access to all company-supported education and training programmes, including literacy classes, vocational and information technology training. Provide equal opportunities for formal and informal networking and mentoring.

Enterprise Development, Supply Chain and Marketing Practices

Try to expand business relationships with women-owned enterprises, including small businesses and women entrepreneurs provided they satisfy all the requisite norms and make the cut. Support gender-sensitive solutions to credit and lending barriers.

Leadership and Engagement

Lead by example – showcase company commitment to gender equality and women's empowerment.Leverage influence, alone or in partnership, to advocate for gender equality Work with community stakeholders, officials and others to eliminate discrimination create opportunities for capable women.

Transparency, Measuring and Reporting

Establish benchmarks that quantify inclusion of women and all levels.Measure and report on progress, both internally and externally, using data disaggregated by sex.Incorporate gender markers into on-going reporting obligations.

Translate Principles into Practice

Prepare resource guides on how to engage women in business operations. Attract and retain highly skilled woman professionals and based on these findings, work to change company culture and policies through leadership and board involvement. Implement an integrated, comprehensive approach to women's advancement through programmes recognizing woman employees' accomplishments and supporting women's advancement in the company through wide-ranging initiatives. Identify concerns of women employees and in response organizes trainings and programmes for capacity building through a range of targeted policies and programmes, The Government has numerous initiatives aimed at supporting women in business, including an online platform to help women connect with other women in business internationally to share information, research and career advice. Recognizing the expanding role of women entrepreneurs, banks SIDBI and some banks as SBI, ICICI have launched specialized financial services, microfinance opportunities and business loans and also provides an online resource centre for women entrepreneurs running small and medium sized enterprises. The internet enables women producers of raw materials in developing countries to trade directly with the manufacturer, thus improving their income by reducing the number of intermediaries in the supply chain.

Things to Consider

Is the stated commitment to advancing equality and promoting non-discrimination and fairness prominently featured on the company's website, in company recruiting materials and corporate sustainability reports?Is there a designated board level individual who champions the organisation's gender equality policies and plans? Are there training, including for male leaders, on the importance of women's participation and inclusion?.Does the company's annual report or sustainability report include leadership statements on reaching gender equality goals.

Women and the Business Case

Investing in women can yield a significant 'gender dividend', according to a 2011 Deloitte report urging the public and private sectors to reap this benefit by investing in women and bringing them into leadership positions. The report highlighted the growing power of women consumers – already controlling roughly US$20 trillion of total consumer spending globally and influencing upto 80 per cent of buying decisions.

A 2011 report from the International Labour Organization (ILO) and Asian Development Bank (ADB) revealed that a gender equality gap in employment rates for women as compared to men cost Asia $47 billion annually – fully 45 per cent of women remained outside the workplace compared to 19 per cent of men.

In 2007, Goldman Sachs reported that different countries and regions of the world could dramatically increase GDP simply by reducing the gap in employment rates between men and women; the Eurozone could increase GDP by 13 per cent; Japan by 16 per cent; the US by 9 per cent.

Education

About two thirds of the estimated 776 million adults – or 16 per cent of the world's adult population – who lack basic literacy skill are women. In developing countries, nearly 1 out of 5 girls who enrols in primary school does not complete her primary education.

The Women's Learning Partnership (WLP) estimates that worldwide, for every year beyond fourth grade that girls attend school, wages rise 20 per cent, child deaths drop 10 per cent and family size drops 20 per cent.

Empowerment

Empowerment means that people both women and men – can take control over their lives: set their own agendas, gain skills (or have their own skills and acknowledgement recognised), increase self-confidence, solve problems, and develop self-reliance. It is both a process and an outcome.

Gender

Gender refers to the array of socially constructed roles and relationships, personality traits, attitudes behaviours , values, relative power and influence that society ascribes to the two sexes on a differential basis. Whereas biological sex is determined by genetic and anatomical characteristics, gender is an acquired identity that is learned, changes overtime, and varies widely within and across cultures. Gender is relational and refers not simply to women or men but to the relationship between them.

Gender Equality

Gender equality describes the concept that all human beings, both women and men, are free to develop their personal abilities and make choices without the limitations set by stereotypes rigid gender roles, or prejudices. Gender equality means that the different behaviours, aspirations and needs of women and men are considered, valued and favoured equally. It does not mean that women and men have to become the same, but that their rights, responsibilities and opportunities will not depend on whether they are born female or male.

Gender Equity

Gender equity means that women and men are treated fairly according to their respective needs. This may include equal treatment or treatment that is different but considered equivalent in terms of rights, benefits, obligations and opportunities. In the development context, a gender equity goal often requires built-in measures to compensate for the historical and social disadvantages of women.

Gender Perspective/'Gender Lens'

A gender perspective/'gender lens' can be defined as a focus that brings a framework of analysis in order to assess how women and men affect and are affected differently by policies, programmes, projects and activities. It enables recognition that relationships between women and men can vary depending on the context. A gender perspective takes into account gender roles, social and economic relationships and needs, access to resources, and other constraints and opportunities imposed by society or culture, age, religion and/or ethnicity on both women and men.

Gender Mainstreaming

Gender mainstreaming is the process of assessing the implications for women and men of any planned action, including legislation, policies or programmes, in any area and at all levels. It is a strategy for making women's as well as men's concerns and experiences an integral dimension in the design, implementation, monitoring and evaluation of policies and programmes in all political, economic and social spheres, such that inequality between women and men is not perpetuated.

These principles draw on the Womens Empowerment Pronciples Equality means Business of the UN Global Compact and UN Women.

If we consider the situation of women in India since economic liberalisation we find us under.

EDUCATION

The level of women's education in India witnessed a sharp rise between 2001 and 2011, with 116 per cent more women passing out as graduates or above compared to a just 65 per cent increase among men. There was also a spike in women completing post-graduation (151 per cent) and those earning professional and technical degrees (196 per cent), key findings of Census 2011, released on Friday, reveal.

In 2011, the country had over 68 million people who were graduates or more qualified. This is over 8 per cent of 838 million people who were 15 years of age or older. A decade ago, this proportion was about 7 per cent. Those with technical degrees (or equivalent) now number 12 million compared to about 5 million in 2001. However, this is a minuscule 1.4 per cent of the total 15+ years population Census 2011 has also released data for educational level for all the people who were seven years or above of age, that is, it includes schoolchildren. The drive for girls to be educated becomes

Position between 2001-2011

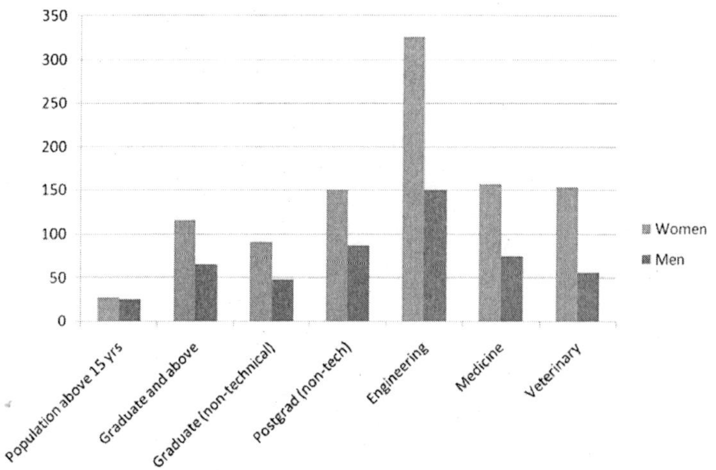

immediately apparent: the number of girls at the mid-school level is up 64 per cent, at matric or secondary level by 50 per cent and at senior secondary level by a whopping 146 per cent. women engineers grew by 326 per cent in these years. In 2001, there were only about 4.8 lakh women engineers. This has exploded to over 20 lakh now. Engineering has for long been dominated by men — there are over 52 lakh men in the profession, more than twice the number of women engineers.

Overall, engineering and related technological degrees appear to be the most popular courses because the number of such graduates has jumped up by a massive 182 per cent in a decade. This may, of course, lead to saturation of the market, experts feel, though the IT sector is still an attractive proposition for women. Though there is a gap between the educational attainments of men and women. Women are moving forward rapidly to close this gap.

There appears to be a preference among women to go for technical education as it is seen to help in getting jobs. This is evident from the fact that the number of women with technical diplomas (not degrees) stands at nearly 19 million, up 146 per cent in a decade. Compare this to non-technical diploma which is held by just 0.34 million (3.4 lakh).

The Economic Survey (2015-16) in the chapter on Social Infrastructure, Employment and Human Development on Page No. 211 states that Human Development Report 2015 also gives the Gender Development Index (GDI) for 188 countries. The Human Development Index (HDI) value for females in India is 0.525 in 2014, which remains unchanged in comparison to that in 2013 (table below). As can be seen in the table, except Pakistan, all other four South Asian Countries have reported higher HDI values for females in comparison to India.

Apart from cultural and social factors that prevent women from engaging in economically productive activities outside the

GDI Component Indices of Select Countries 2014

Country	*GDI Value Group 2014*		*HDI Value 2014*		*LED (years) 2014**		*Expected years of schooling 2014**		*Mean years of schooling 2014*		*GNI per capita in ($) 2014*	
	Female	*Male*	*Female*	*Male*	*Female*	*Male*	*Female*	*Male*	*Female*	*Male*	*Female*	*Male*
Sri Lanka	0.948	3	0.730	0.769	78.2	71.5	14.2	13.3	10.7	10.9	5452	14307
China	0.943	3	0.705	0.747	77.3	74.3	13.2	12.9	6.9	8.2	10128	14795
India	0.795	5	0.525	0.660	69.5	66.6	11.3	11.8	3.6	7.2	2116	8656
Bangladesh	0.917	4	0.541	0.590	72.9	70.4	10.3	9.7	4.5	5.5	2278	4083
Pakistan	0.726	5	0.436	0.601	67.2	65.3	7.0	8.5	3.1	6.5	1450	8100

Source: HDR 2015

Notes: Countries are categorised into five groups based on their absolute deviations of HDI values between men and women. Group 5 represents low equality of HD values between men and women with above 10 per cent absolute deviations.

* Data refers to 2014 the most recent year availabel; $: Gross National Income (GNI) per capita is based on 2011 dollar purchasing Power Parity (PPP).

household, the lack of education and skills restricts them from participating in economic activity. Therefore, in the present cultural context, and with a large proportion of women in the growing population of India, it is necessary to address the sources of gender inequality to enable women to contribute more fully to India's Economic Resurgence.

Over the years female employment situation has improved. In 2015, 22 per cent of total employees in the scheduled commercial banks are female employee as compared to 13.6 per cent in 1996. Also bank (SCB) credit to female has also increased to 17 per cent in 2015 as compared to 6 per cent in 1996.

NSSO data reveals female employment has increased in case of regular wage / salaried (organized sector) over the year.

Females get less wages than Males. However, disparities, in terms of wage (wage to female as a percentage to wage to male) is less pronounced in urban area and the gap is closing.

1. Scheduled commercial Bank (as on 31st March): Employment and deployment of credit

Year	*Proportion of female employees (in per cent)*	*Proportion of credit accounts held by females*
1996	13.6	6.36
2010	16.6	14.22
2011	17.8	15.06
2012	18.3	15.82
2013	19.1	16.89
2014	22.2	16.91
2015	21.7	16.46

**Source:* BSR

2. Unemployment rates (per 1000 persons in the labour force) usual status

	Rural		Urban	
	Male	Female	Male	Female
1987-88	28	35	61	83
2004-05	21	31	44	91
2009-10	29	24	30	70
2011-12	21	29	32	66

* *Source*: NSSO.

3. per 1000 distribution: National Sample Survey, GoI

	rural females			urban females		
	self employeed	*regular wage/ salaried employees*	*casual labour*	*self employeed*	*regular wage/ salaried employees*	*casual labour*
1987-88	549	49	402	393	342	265
1993-94	513	34	453	372	355	273
1999-00	500	39	461	384	385	231
2004-05	564	48	389	404	422	174
2009-10	503	55	442	354	444	202
2011-12	535	76	389	368	487	146

* *Source*: NSSO

4. Average wage/ salary earnings per day received by regular wage /salaried employeespf age group 15-59 years: National Sample Survey, GoI

	rural			*urban*		
year	*male*	*female*	*female/male*	*male*	*female*	*female/male*
1993-94	58.48	34.89	59.66	78.12	62.31	79.76
2004-05	144.93	85.53	59.01	203.28	153.19	75.36
2009-10	249.15	155.87	62.56	377.16	308.79	81.87
2011-12	322.28	201.56	62.54	469.87	366.15	77.93

* *Source:* NSSO

Selected Indicators on Status of Men and Women

Indicators	***Male***	***Female***
Literacy Rate (per cent) Census 2011	82.14	65.46
Maternal mortality ratio (per100,000 live births) SRS 2009-	10	212
Sex Ratio Census 2011	1000	940
Child Sex Ratio (0-6 years) Census 2011	1000	914
Worker Population ratios (Per1000)	819	336
MPs in Lok Sabha (per cent)	89.8	10.82 per cent

India is amongst the fastest growing countries in the world today, with an envisaged GDP growth rate of more than 7 per cent This high level of growth can, however, be sustained only when all sections of the society, specially women are treated as equal partners in the development process. It is well recognised that societies which discriminate by gender tend to experience less rapid economic growth and poverty reduction than societies which do not. Empowerment of women is a socio-political ideal, encompassing notions of dignity and equality, envisioned in relation to the wider framework of women's rights. It is a process of gaining control over self, over resources and over existing societal perceptions and attitudes and would be achieved only when an improvement in the 'condition' of women is accompanied by an advancement in their 'position' by regarding men and women more equally. Gender equality and empowerment is, thus, a core development goal .Empowerment is an enabling process which leads to economic and social transformation. Government is seeking to operationalise this approach through legislative and programmatic interventions as well as by mainstreaming gender into the development planning process. The SEBI directive to have at least at last one woman on Company Boards is expected to have a significant impact on the economic advancement of women.

Since national budgets impact men and women differently through the pattern of resource allocation, the scope and coverage of schemes for women and child development have been expanded with progressive increase in Plan expenditure under various Plan schemes, and gender budgeting (GB).The allocation for GB as a percentage of total have has increased from 2.7 per cent in 2005-06 to 5.91 per cent in 2012-13.

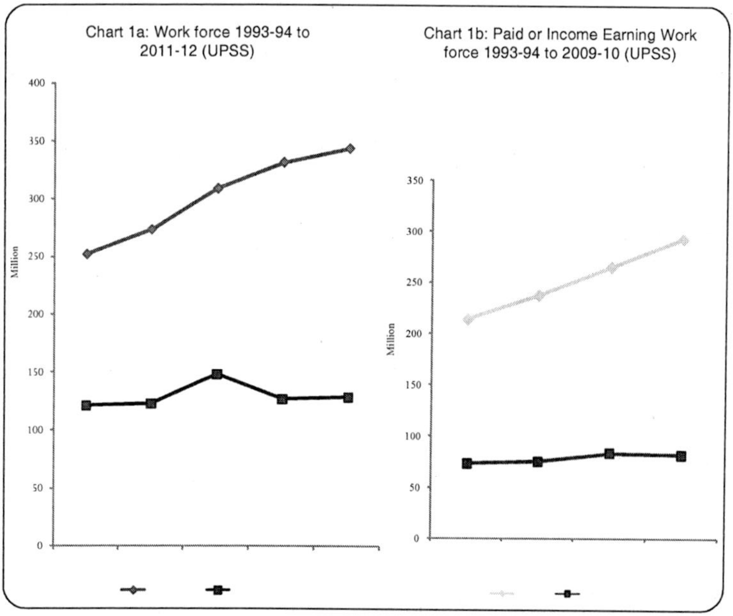

Chart 1: Growing gender gap in Employment (a reflection of economic disparity

The *Women's Economic Opportunity Index* is a pilot effort by Economic Intelligence Unit to assess the laws, regulations, practices, and attitudes that affect women workers and entrepreneurs. It uses 26 indicators, selected and validated by a panel of gender experts, to evaluate every aspect of the economic and social value chain for women, from fertility to retirement. By exploring the binding constraints that women

Industry	***No. of Paid/Income Earning Female Workers (UPSS) {Excluding unpaid helpers} [in millions]***				***No. of Female Workers (UPSS){including unpaid} [in millions]***				
	1993-94	*1999-00*	*2004-05*	*2009-10*	*1993-94*	*1999-00*	*2004-05*	*2009-10*	*2011-12*
Agriculture	52.8	52.7	52.7	47.8	94.2	92.4	107.8	87.6	81.0
Manufacturing	7.9	7.6	11.6	10.8	11.5	12.4	13.1	13.8	17.3
Construction	1.5	1.9	2.7	6.5	1.6	2.0	2.7	6.5	7.9
All Workers	73.7	75.2	83.7	82.2	121.7	123.0	148.6	127.5	129.1

face, it points to steps governments can take to improve opportunities for women and boost overall economic performance.

The Women's Economic Opportunity Index is a dynamic quantitative and qualitative scoring model constructed from 26 indicators that measure specific attributes of the environment for women employees and entrepreneurs in 113 economies.

Economic Disparity and Women: Global Scenario

- The Gender Inequality Index (2013) shows that the Sub-Saharan Africa and Asian countries have maximum Gender Inequality followed by Arab States. Among Countries Netherlands is the best in Gender Equality.
- Yemen and Afghanistan are the worst performing countries in the world in terms of Gender Equality. Significant gaps remain in some regions. In South and West Asia, 66 per cent of out-of-school children are girls. Gender differences in labour force participation rates, unemployment rates and gender wage gaps are a persistent feature of global labour markets. Nearly two thirds of all employed women in developing countries work either as contributing family workers or as own-account workers, extremely vulnerable employment which lacks security and benefits. The Global Gender Gap Index (2013) ranks Iceland as the best in terms of Gender Gap i.e. having the least Gender disparity in terms of economic participation and opportunities, educational attainment, health and survival and political empowerment. Yemen stands last at ranking of 136 in Global Gender Gap Index. In terms of Economic Participation and opportunities, Norway ranks first, while Syria fairs the worst with ranking of 136. Pakistan, Saudi Arabia, Algeria and Yemen are other countries with poor Economic Participation and opportunities. While Indian and Chinese men exhibit

similar work participation rates, Indian women substantially lag behind the Chinese women. In South Asia, North Africa and West Asia, employment opportunities remain very low. The *Women's Economic Opportunity Index* computed by the Economist Intelligence Unit shows that Sweden, Belgium and Norway occupy the top spots in the Index. These countries have particularly open labour markets for women, high levels of educational achievement, and liberal legal and social regimes. Hong Kong (China) performs best in the Asia region, ranking in the top 25 per cent in most categories. Mauritius is Africa's best finisher; its labour policies are among the most favourable to women in the region. Excluding Canada and the US, Brazil edges Chile and Mexico for the best score in the Americas. Eastern European countries, especially Bulgaria, have particularly balanced labour-law protections.

Proportion of seats held by women national parliament (per cent)

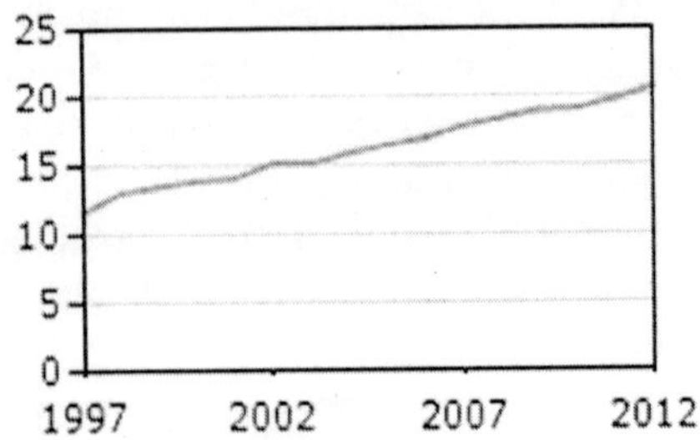

Only 20.8 per cent of the seats are held by women in national Parliaments (2012).

Source World Development Indicators

- Barriers to empowerment is one of the reasons for economic disparity in India. Inequality in labour

> opportunities and outcomes can occur because a disproportionate share of unpaid work falls on women. Social protection schemes, such as the provision of maternity leave and benefits, help to mitigate this.
>
> Deep-rooted ideologies of gender bias and discrimination like the confinement of women to the private domestic realm, restrictions on their mobility, poor access to health services, nutrition, education and employment, and exclusion from the public and political sphere continue to daunt women across the country.
>
> Women often face greater difficulties than men in securing credit due to a lack of collateral. Women's access to property is restricted either by law or custom in many countries, leaving them with few assets.

India can increase its 2025 gross domestic product (GDP), estimated at $4.83 trillion, by between 16 per cent and 60 per cent simply by enabling women to participate in the economy on par with men, according to a new study by the McKinsey Global Institute (MGI).

The upper end of that range—if everything works out the way it should, or a so-called full-potential scenario—could add $2.9 trillion to India's 2025 GDP. The lower end—the so-called best-in-region scenario in which all countries only match the rate of improvement of the best country in the region—could add $700 billion.

That holds true for the world as well, according to *The Power of Parity: How equality for women could drive $12 trillion in global growth*, released on 24 September.

Equal participation by women would add as much as $28 trillion, or 26 per cent, to the world's 2025 GDP in a best-case scenario—roughly equivalent to the size of the combined US and Chinese economies today—or 11 per cent in a best-in-region scenario.

Conducted in 95 countries, home to 93 per cent of the world's women, the study places a definitive value to increased women's participation in the workplace. India has one of the world's largest gender gaps when it comes to labour force participation, with women accounting for 23-24 per cent of the total labour force and generating a mere 17 per cent of the share of GDP, finds the MGI study India could add 60 per cent to the GDP by just bridging the gender gap.

If we consider the situation of women in India since economic liberalisation we find that women have contributed significantly to economic growth and they have made positive contributions to India's Development.

Chapter 1

Corporate Governance

A leadership position implies, taking a leap of faith across the chasm with followers in trim. It does not mean, sitting forever gridlocked, at the middle management level drawing up "how to do it" plans. To leap across the chasm, figuratively, risking the lives of others implies a certain understanding and knowledge of the terrain. This knowledge ensures that we, women, will land on our feet and so will all others who follow us. We will always land feet first on the ground. When needed we will be able to soar and rise. To do this we have to cultivate the capabilities, which enable us to do so. SEBI vide amendment to Section 49 of the Companies Act has mandated that every Company must have a woman on Board and failure to achieve this will result in penalty. Being elevated as members of Corporate Boards is just one way women can contribute to development and economic resurgence of the country.

Having women on Board introduces an element of gender diversity on the board. It mainstreams the marginalised women and gives them a significant voice. They have an opportunity to influence decisions that affect the Company that affects the Country. A representation-based approach is really only quarter of a solution for ensuring gender diversity on corporate boards. Securities Exchange Board of India (SEBI) has introduced a graded penalty system for companies that fail to comply with the requirement of having at least a woman director on the Boards. This has resulted in a scramble to fill up positions over the past year. The appointment of 1,800 women directors on boards of companies in a short span of time is not a matter of self-congratulation but a pyrrhic victory. Several large and well-known companies have resorted to close familial and figurehead appointments. These allow Companies to tick the box and to fulfil the formalities by complying with the letter of the Law and not the spirit of the Law. Where does this lead us? As far as gender empowerment is concerned – this does not lead women anywhere. The only purpose this ritualistic exercise subserves is to block the progress of meritorious women from ascending to the boards of companies, where they remain grossly under-represented. It is important that a meritocracy of women leaders fill up Corporate Board level positions. These leaders need to possess talent, trustworthiness and expertise in abundant measure. These women should also be independent Directors unrelated to the promoters and with substantial stake but not substantial shareholding in the companies they govern to allow for more independent decision making. Gender diversity, brings a different feel to the Boardroom. The presence of women on Company board's helps to enhance Corporate Governance. Hence, we begin with a discussion of **Corporate Governance. Where and when did Corporate Governance become part of mainstream discourse and what does this imply?**

The Sarbanes-Oxley Act of 2002 (often shortened to **SOX**) is legislation passed by the US Congress to protect shareholders and the public from accounting errors and fraudulent practices in the enterprise, as well as improve the accuracy of corporate disclosures. SOX is the basis of much of corporate governance discourse. It was enacted on 30th, July, 2002 nine months after the first announcement of Enron problems. As a concept, contemporary corporate governance came to the forefront in 1992 with the submission of the Cadbury report in the UK. Corporate Governance quite simply, implies the policies, procedures and rules governing the relationships between the shareholders, directors and managers of a company. These relationships are defined in terms of extant applicable laws and the corporate charter, read with the company's bye-laws, and formal policies.

Definition of Corporate Governance

The SEBI Committee on Corporate Governance defines corporate governance as "the mechanisms, processes and relationships which govern the interactions between stakeholders and by which corporations are controlled and directed." This definition implies an acceptance by management of the inalienable rights of shareholders as the true owners of the corporations and of their own role as trustees on behalf of the shareholders. It is rooted in commitment to values, ethical business conduct and draws a distinction between personal and corporate fund allocation in the management of the company.

Governance structures thus serve to identify the distribution of rights and responsibilities, among different participants in the corporation such as the board of directors, managers, shareholders, creditors, auditors, regulators, and others and include the rules and procedures for making decisions in corporate affairs. Corporate governance includes the processes through which corporations' objectives are set and pursued in the context of the social, regulatory and market environment. Governance mechanisms include monitoring the actions, policies and decisions of corporations and their agents. Interest in the corporate governance practices of modern corporations, particularly in relation to accountability, increased following the collapses of large corporations during 2001–2002, most of which involved accounting fraud; and then the financial crisis of 2008 brought the need for corporate governance into even sharper focus.

The Cadbury Report was the result of several high profile company collapses. It concerned itself primarily with protecting weak and widely dispersed shareholders against the pursuit of self-interests by Directors and managers, to cope with the failures of the corporate sector worldwide in the late 1980s and the early 1990s. The Financial Reporting Council, the London Stock of Exchange and the accountancy profession, set up the Cadbury Committee with the main aim of addressing the financial aspects of Corporate Governance. The terms of reference of the Cadbury committee included:

(i) Redress the low level of confidence both in financial reporting and in the ability of auditors to provide the safeguards which the users of company's reports sought and expected;

(ii) Review the structure, rights and roles of board of directors, shareholders and auditors by making them more effective and accountable;

(iii) Address various aspects of the accountancy profession and make appropriate recommendations, wherever necessary;

(iv) Raise the standard of corporate governance; etc. Keeping this in view, the Committee published its final report on 1st December 1992. The Cadbury Committee report laid down a code of best practices specifying the Role of the Board of Directors and the role of Non-Executive Directors, specifying their remuneration and addressing questions of financial reporting and financial controls. The report is divisible in three parts. It recommends - **Reviewing the structure and responsibilities of Boards of Directors and recommending a Code of Best Practice** - The boards of all listed companies should comply with the Code of Best Practice. All listed companies should make a statement about their compliance with the Code in their report and accounts as well as give reasons for any areas of non-compliance. The Code of Best Practice is segregated into four sections and their respective recommendations are:-

1. **Board of Directors** - The board should meet regularly, retain full and effective control over the

company and monitor the executive management. There should be a clearly accepted division of responsibilities at the head of a company, which will ensure a balance of power and authority, such that no one individual has unfettered powers of decision. Where the chairperson is also the chief executive, it is essential that there should be a strong and independent element on the board, with a recognised senior member. Besides, all directors should have access to the advice and services of the company secretary, who is responsible to the Board for ensuring that board procedures are observed and applicable rules and regulations are complied with.

2. **Non-Executive Directors** - The non-executive directors should bring independent judgement to bear on issues of strategy, performance, resources, including key appointments, and standards of conduct. The majority of non-executive directors should be independent of management and free from any business or other relationship with the company which could materially interfere with the exercise of their independent judgement, apart from their fees and shareholding.
3. **Executive Directors** - There should be full and clear disclosure of directors' total emoluments and those of the chairperson and highest-paid directors, including pension contributions and stock options, in the company's annual report, including separate figures for salary and performance-related pay.
4. **Financial Reporting and Controls** - It is the duty of the board to present a balanced and understandable assessment of their company's position, in reporting of financial statements, for providing true and fair picture of financial reporting. The directors

should report that the business is a going concern, with supporting assumptions or qualifications as necessary. The board should ensure that an objective and professional relationship is maintained with the auditors.

Considering the role of Auditors and addressing a number of recommendations to the Accountancy Profession

Annual audit is a cornerstone of corporate governance. It provides an external and objective check on the financial statements prepared and presented by the directors of the company. The Cadbury Committee recommended that a professional and objective relationship between the board of directors and auditors is maintained, to provide a true and fair view of the company's financial statements. Auditors' role is to design audit in such a manner so that it provides a reasonable assurance that the financial statements are free of material misstatements. Further, there is a need to develop effective accounting standards, which provide important reference points against which auditors exercise their professional judgement. Secondly, every listed company should form an audit committee that gives the auditors direct access to the non-executive members of the board. The Committee further recommended for a regular rotation of audit partners to prevent unhealthy relationship between auditors and the management. It also recommended for disclosure of payments to the auditors for non-audit services to the company. The Accountancy Profession, in conjunction with representatives of preparers of accounts, should take the lead in:-

(i) developing a set of criteria for assessing effectiveness;

(ii) developing guidance for companies on the form in which directors should report; and

(iii) developing guidance for auditors on relevant audit procedures and the form in which auditors should report. However, it should continue to improve its standards and procedures.

Dealing with the Rights and Responsibilities of Shareholders

The shareholders, as owners of the company, elect the directors to run the business on their behalf and hold them accountable for progress. They appoint the auditors to provide an external check on the directors' financial statements. The Committee's report places particular emphasis on the need for fair and accurate reporting of a company's progress to its shareholders, which is the responsibility of the board. The institutional investors/shareholders are encouraged to make greater use of their voting rights and take positive interest in the board functioning. Both shareholders and boards of directors should consider how the effectiveness of general meetings is increased as well as how to strengthen the accountability of boards of directors to shareholders.

The Directors are the – Guardians of the Company's assets for the Shareholders and the Managers who use the Company's assets. It concerns itself with Public Ltd Companies and came to the fore with the dramatic collapse of companies like Enron. Its characteristics are FAIT - Fairness Accountability Independence and Transparency. It Protects Shareholders' rights and ensure equitable treatment of all shareholders especially of minorities. It needs to have in place an effective mechanism for grievance redress and as determined by Its shareholders a mode of penalty for violation of the same must underpin its actions. If - the business of business is just business. Business must reward and pay back shareholders who contribute to its capital with adequate returns. Thus, as a measure of Accountability it must ensure that management is accountable to the Board. It must make certain that the ultimate accountability of the Board is to the shareholders. While conflicts of interest are bound to be there, to ensure that the company works in an effective and ethical manner, procedures and structures need to be clearly laid down to minimise and mitigate completely conflicts of interest. Independent Directors and Advisers i.e. free from the influence of others. Ensure timely, accurate disclosure on all material matters, including the financial situation, performance, corporate ownership.

What are the characteristics of Corporate Governance?

The characteristics of corporate governance are:

Good Board Practices, appropriate Board procedures, director Remuneration in line with best practice. Board self-evaluation and trainings conducted.

Control Environment: Internal control procedures need to be set out with a risk management and mitigation framework present and disaster recovery systems are in place. Business continuity procedures in place. Independent external auditor conducts audits. An Independent audit committees established. Internal Audit Function Management, Information systems, are established along with the Compliance Function.

Transparent disclosure: Policy on disclosure of Financial Information laid down and disclosed, likewise on the disclosure of Non-Financial Information disclosed. Financial Statements Financial information is prepared according to International Financial Reporting Standards (IFRS). Date - The Company publishes its Annual accounts and shareholder report in the form of a high-quality annual report which is published accompanied by Web-based disclosure.

Well-defined shareholder rights imply that the Minority shareholder rights are formalised and that they have a right to fairly exercise these in well-organised shareholder meetings conducted as per prescribed periodicity and there is a clearly understood policy on related party transactions with effective Board commitment and governance. There also needs to be a policy covering extraordinary transactions those that are exceptions are which these are out of the ordinary, and are contingent on special events. It is extremely significant that a defined and explicit dividend policy is determined.

Sound Corporate Governance Practices - The Board needs to discuss corporate governance issues and create a corporate governance committee for adequate follow up. The company requires a corporate governance champion. A corporate governance improvement plan needs to be created. Appropriate resources need to be committed to foster corporate governance initiatives. Policies and procedures need formalisation. These require effective dissemination so there is awareness and sensitisation of the relevant officials in this regard. A corporate governance code has to be developed. A code of ethics needs to be in place. The company should gain recognition as a corporate governance leader. Corporate Governance is by way of legislation or best practice Code. US adopted legislation in 2002 - Sarbanes Oxley Act. Most other developed and emerging market countries have adopted best practice Codes e.g. Combined Code in the UK, The Cromme Code in Germany. These Codes are voluntary adopted though they are enforceable by shareholders. Most of them operate on a 'comply or explain' approach. The Media also play a part in highlighting good or bad practices.

What are the gains of corporate governance adoption to the company? Firstly, all companies need finance a sound corporate governance code facilitates better access to external

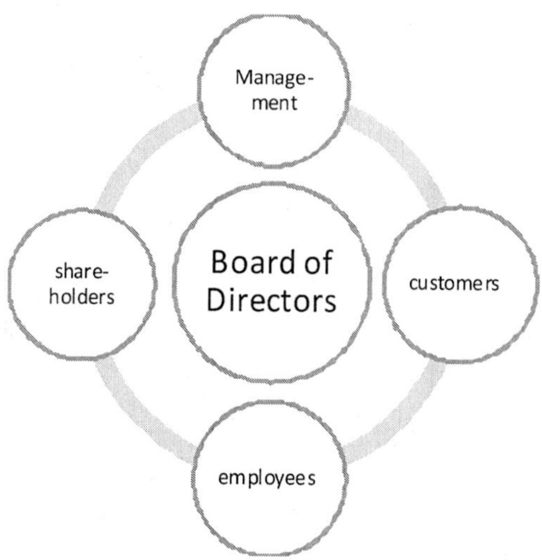

finance. This lowers the costs of capital by reducing the interest rates on loans especially as in the present scenario companies find external commercial borrowing a cheaper option. This leads to improved company performance – sustainability, higher valuation of the firm and consequently better Return on Assigned capital and Return on Investment and Return on Equity improved share performance. It significantly reduces the risks of corporate crisis and other scandals.

This spirit of effective corporate governance has to percolate from the Management to shareholders, customers and employees. To sum up the important thing as Lord Acton had phrased, it is that "Power corrupts and absolute power corrupts absolutely". Thus, the Gender Diverse Board of Directors of the company should comprise of a mix of Executive, Non-Executive members, their roles, responsibilities should be specified, and the business must be conducted in an ethical manner.

Corporate Governance defined as "A set of systems, processes and principles which ensure that a company is governed in the best interest of all stakeholders." It ensures Commitment to values and ethical conduct of business; Transparency in business transactions; Statutory and legal compliance; adequate disclosures and Effective decision-making to achieve corporate objectives. In other words, Corporate Governance is about promoting corporate fairness, transparency and accountability. Good Corporate Governance is simply Good Business. **Companies within a business case also link Corporate Governance to the concept of corporate social responsibility (CSR) corporate social responsibility (CSR, also called corporate conscience, corporate citizenship, social performance, or sustainable responsible business/Responsible Business) is a form of self-regulation**. CSR policy functions as a built-in, self-regulating mechanism whereby a business monitors and ensures its active compliance with the spirit of the law, ethical standards, and international practice. In some models, a firm's implementation of CSR goes beyond compliance and engages in "actions that appear to further some social good, beyond the interests of the firm and that which is required by law." CSR is a process with the aim of excapting the responsibility for the company's actions and encourage a positive impact through its activities on the environment, consumers, employees, communities, and all other members with whom interactions take place in the wider public spaces and who can consequently be considered stakeholders.

The term "corporate social responsibility" became popular in the 1960s and has remained a term used indiscriminately by many to cover legal and moral responsibility more narrowly construed.

Proponents argue that corporations make more long-term profits by operating with a perspective, while critics argue that CSR distracts from the economic role of businesses. McWilliams and Siegel's article (2000) published in the Strategic Management Journal cited by over 1000 academics, compared existing studies of the relationship between social and financial performance. They concluded that the contradictory results of previous studies reporting positive, negative, and neutral financial impact were due to empirical analysis which had seriously flawed premises to begin with. McWilliams and Siegel demonstrated that when the model is specific that is, when you control for research and development investment, an important determinant of financial performance, CSR has a neutral impact on financial outcomes.

Why are we in India focussing on Corporate Social Responsibility at this juncture of the country's development?

In August 2013, the Indian Parliament passed the Indian Companies Act, 2013 (the "New Act"), which has replaced the Companies Act of 1956. The New Act has made far-reaching changes affecting company formation, administration and governance, and it has increased shareholder control over board decisions. The New Act is under implementation in stages.

Corporate Social Responsibility

One of the New Act's changes—which came into effect on 1st April 2014—has been to impose compulsory corporate social responsibility obligations ("CSR") upon Indian companies and foreign companies operating in India. These obligations mainly come in the form of mandatory amounts. Companies must contribute to resolving social problems. This is a wholly new requirement; although companies were allowed within limits, to make charitable contributions in the past, the New Act is essentially a self-administered tax. The Ministry of Corporate Affairs recently published, i.e. "notified," detailed rules implementing the CSR requirements.

Entities Covered by the CSR Obligations

The threshold coverage levels for CSR are low. Companies are subject to the CSR requirements if they have, for any financial year:

- a net worth of at least Rs 5 billion (approximately US$80 million);
- a turnover of at least Rs 10 billion (approximately US$160 million); or
- Net profits of at least Rs 50 million (approximately US [$800,000).

Companies meeting these thresholds are required to develop a CSR policy, spend a minimum amount on CSR activities and report on these activities, or prepare to explain why they did not do so. Women have an important role in ensuring that all the CSR Obligations are fulfilled.

Required Amount of CSR Spending

An entity or business that meets these specified thresholds must spend on CSR activities no less than two per cent of its average *net profit* for its preceding three financial years. *Net profit* means a company's profits as per its profit and loss account prepared in accordance with the New Act, but excludes profits from a company's operations outside India or dividends received from an Indian company that has itself met its CSR requirements.

Permitted Corporate Social Responsibility (CSR) Activities

There is a long list of permissible areas for CSR funding. They include such purposes as ending hunger and poverty; promoting public health; supporting education; addressing gender inequality; protecting the environment; and funding cultural initiatives and the arts.

All CSR funds must be spent in India. The New Act encourages companies to spend their CSR funds in the areas where they operate, but money cannot be spent on activities undertaken that are part of the normal course of the company's business or on projects for the exclusive benefit of employees or their family members.

Contributions of any amount to a political party are not a permitted CSR activity. However, the New Act has an exception allowing companies to use their CSR funds to support development projects initiated by the Prime Minister or Central Government. It is important to note, as discussed further below, that such projects in India have had a troubling tendency to become vehicles for political patronage, and they can raise legal issues in other jurisdictions if they come to be seen as political payoffs.

The Government of India with the pasane of the new Act, has made CSR spending compulsory. While the initiative is good all companies should have a policy on CSR, however, there has to be a clear distinction between the CSR initiatives and the business strategy of any company. If companies for furthering their business cause use CSR as a tool, then the entire spirit with which the act is passed is dampened.

The Securities and Exchange Board of India has a governance role on the Indian Stock Exchange it has promulgated Clause 49 of the Listing Agreement to the comes into effect from 31 December 2005. This is designed to ensure corporate Governance in all the Listed companies.

Corporate hierarchies envisage the following two types of companies:

(i) Companies managed by the Board of Directors

(ii) Companies controlled and managed through a Managing Director, the whole-time director or manager, subject to the guidance of the Board of Directors.

- As per Clause 49, of the SEBI listing agreement where a Company is managed through an Executive Chairman, at least 50 per cent of the board should comprise independent directors. In the case of a company with a non-executive Chairman, at least one-third of the board should comprise independent directors.
- It is essential for chief executives and chief financial officers to establish and maintain internal controls and implement remedial and risk mitigation models for addressing deficiencies in internal controls.
- Clause VI (ii) of Clause 49 of SEBI listing agreement requires all companies to submit a quarterly compliance report to the Stock Exchange, in the prescribed form. The clause also requires that there be a separate section on corporate governance in the Annual Report with a detailed compliance report.
- The clause mandates composition of an Audit committee; one of the directors is required to be financially literate.
- It is mandatory for all listed companies to comply with the clause by 31 December 2005.

Clause 49 of the guidelines on Corporate Governance as amended on 29 October 2004 has effected major changes in the definition of independent directors. It has strengthened the responsibilities of audit committees, improving quality of financial disclosures, including those relating to related party transactions and proceeds from public/ rights/ preferential issues. It requires Boards to adopt formal code of conduct. The Chief Executive Officer and the Chief Financial Officer require certification of financial statements and for improving disclosures to shareholders. Certain non-mandatory clauses like policy for protection of Whistle Blowers and restriction of the term of independent directors have also been included.

The term 'Clause 49' refers to clause number 49 of the Listing Agreement between a company and the stock exchanges on which it is listed (the Listing Agreement is identical for all Indian stock exchanges, including the National Stock Exchange and the Bombay Stock Exchange). This clause is a recent addition to the Listing Agreement and was inserted as late as 2000 consequent to the recommendations of the Kumarmangalam Birla Committee on Corporate Governance constituted by the Securities Exchange Board of India (SEBI) in 1999.

Clause 49, when it was first added, was intended to introduce some basic corporate governance practices in Indian companies and brought in a number of key changes in governance and disclosures (many of which we take for granted today). It specified the minimum number of independent directors required on the board of a company. The setting up of an Audit committee, and a Shareholders' Grievance committee, among others, were made mandatory as were the Management's Discussion and Analysis (MD&A) section and the Report on Corporate Governance in the Annual Report, and disclosures of fees paid to non-executive directors. A limit was placed on the number of committees that a director could serve on.

The Securities Exchange Board of India in late 2002, constituted a Committee under Mr Narayan Murthy popularly known as the Narayan Murthy Committee to assess the adequacy of current corporate governance practices and to suggest improvements. Based on the recommendations of this committee, SEBI issued a modified Clause 49 on 29 October 2004 (the 'revised Clause 49') which came into operation on 1 January 2006.

The revised Clause 49 has suitably pushed forward the original intent of protecting the interests of investors through enhanced governance practices and disclosures. Five broad themes predominate. 1. The criteria of what constitutes independent directors has been specified. 2. The roles and responsibilities of the board stand enhanced. 3. The quality and quantity of disclosures have improved. 4. The roles and responsibilities of the audit committee in all matters relating to internal controls and financial reporting have been consolidated, and 5. The accountability of top management—specifically the CEO and CFO—has been enhanced. Within each of these areas, the revised Clause 49 moves further into the realm of global best practices (and sometimes, even beyond).

By Circular dated 8 April 2008, the Securities and Exchange Board of India amended Clause 49 of the Listing Agreement to extent the 50 per cent independent directors rule to all Boards of Directors where the Non-Executive Chairman is a promoter of the Company or related to the promoters of the company.

At the end of the first India Corporate Week in December 2009, the Ministry of Corporate Affairs issued new Corporate Governance Voluntary Guidelines and new Corporate Social Responsibility Voluntary Guidelines.

Committee, Customer Service Committee, Shareholders Investors Grievance Committee, Share Transfer Committee, Remuneration Committee and so on and so forth and yet the health of PSBs remains a cause for concern.

Corporate governance is an essential element of sound regulatory architecture.

The ***proper*** governance of companies will become as crucial to the world economy as the ***proper governing of countries***. James D. Wolfensohn

To ensure that a company functions in the most efficient manner, it is vital to have a relevant and a rather fail-safe legal mechanism in place. This mechanism comprises suitable rules, regulations, procedures and principles which aim to strike a balance between the interests of the shareholders on the one hand and those of the stakeholders on the other. The management of funds in an ethical manner is one of the various objectives the concept of corporate governance seeks to achieve.

Apart from the evident boons of economic development, concepts of globalisation and ferocious competition also unveil the gruesome likelihood of increased vulnerability to corporate scams, frauds and fiascos. History is replete with instances of corporate debacles not only in India but also across the globe. The failure of Maxwell, BCCI and Polypeck resulted in the formation of Cadbury Committee in the United Kingdom. Collapses such as Worldcom, Xerox, Enron led to the enactment of Sarbanes Oxley Act, 2002. In the wake of corporate massacres, shaken investors had sought an overhaul of regulatory standards.

Corporate governance, a term, which finds a mention in every other business daily, corporate panel discussions and various legislations, is nothing short of a phenomenon. Corporate governance is a multi-pronged approach which aims to focus on principles of accountability, transparency, fairness, responsibility, integrity and disclosure.

Definitions of Corporate Governance

OECD defines corporate governance as involving a set of relationship between a company's management, its board, its shareholders and other stakeholders. Corporate governance also provides the structure through which the objectives and monitoring performance are determines. Good corporate governance should provide proper incentives for the board and management to pursue objectives that are in the interests of the company and shareholders and should facilitate effective monitoring, thereby encouraging firms to use resources more efficiently.

According to World Bank, Corporate Governance is:

- Blend of law, regulation and appropriate voluntary private sector practices.
- Which enable the corporation to attract financial and human capital.
- Perpetuate itself by generating long-term economic value for its shareholders.
- While respecting the interests of stakeholders and society as a whole.

Corporate governance is the way in which boards oversee the running of a company by managers, and the manner in which board members are in turn accountable to shareholders and the company. This has implications for company behaviour towards employees, shareholders, customers and banks. Good corporate governance plays a vital role in underpinning the integrity and efficiency of financial markets. Poor corporate governance weakens a company's potential and at worst can pave the way for financial difficulties and even fraud. Well governed companies, generally outperform other companies and are be able to attract investors whose support can help to finance further growth.

Good governance is integral to the very existence of a company. It inspires and strengthens investor's confidence by ensuring company's commitment to higher growth and profits. Corporate governance thus seeks to achieve following objectives:

(i) That a properly structured Board capable of taking independent and objective decisions is in place at the helm of affairs;

(ii) That the Board is balanced as regards the representation of adequate number of non-executive and independent directors who will take care of the interests and well being of all the stakeholders;

(iii) That the Board adopts transparent procedures and practices and arrives at decisions on the strength of adequate information;

(iv) That the Board has an effective machinery to subserve the concerns of stakeholders;

(v) That the Board keeps the shareholders informed of relevant developments impacting the company;

(vi) That the Board effectively and regularly monitors the functioning of the management team; and

(vii) That the Board remains in effective control of the affairs of the company acts to take the organisation forward, to maximise long-term value and shareholders' wealth.

Corporate governance is defined as the relationship among various participants in determining the direction and performance of corporations (Monks and Minow, 2004:1). The review of Literature reflects that there is no precise definition of what constitutes good corporate governance.

Women Directors need to focus on three main areas

- *Principles:* Accountability, transparency, responsibility and equity or fairness.
- *Mission of the board of directors:* Monitoring, managerial and strategic guidance.
- *Prerequisites:* Directors expertise and qualifications.

Vitality of a good Corporate Governance Regimen. In order to win the confidence of investors, it is essential to have a strong corporate governance regime. A company with a reputation of being ill-managed will certainly not attract investors. A company, which does not abide by disclosure, transparency, auditing and accountability norms, as mandated by the law, would end up discouraging investments. Any lax view of corporate governance measures ultimately affects corporate growth. The detrimental effects and cracks would ultimately show on the economic health of the country.

The principles of Corporate Governance that can serve as a guide for Women Directors

Transparency, adequate disclosure, effective decision-making, statutory and legal compliance, accountability are the principles which lend sanctity to the concept of corporate governance. Good corporate governance is a mechanism, whereby, the management aims to increase the long-term value for its shareholders and at the same time protect the interest of stakeholders. These objectives are secured through efficacious corporate performance, accountability and a defined sense of responsibility. The goal of increasing the wealth of the shareholders has to be achieved in an ethical manner without jeopardising stakeholders' interest. In the environment of globalisation and ever increasing competitiveness, corporate governance seeks to create trust and confidence among conflicting factions.

Corporate practices in the matter of disclosure, transparency, group accounting, role of directors, degree of accountability to the shareholders, lenders and overall public good are some of the critical issues which require a fresh and closer look. A framework for addressing concerns public good, such as regard for environment, overall conservation of resources, cost effective managerial input—all these would, among other things form part of the core of corporate governance. Government can play a catalytic role in creating the environment for quality governance through an appropriate regulatory framework. Corporate leadership and its mindset would determine the sort of governance that would ultimately evolve.

There are four governance principles responsibility, accountability, fairness and transparency.

Responsibility: Responsibility refers to the recognition of all stakeholders' rights such as provided by law and the promotion of active cooperation between the company and main stakeholders to create wealth and sustainable enterprises. In addition, responsibility implies that the board ensures corporate compliance with laws and regulations that reflect the values of society. Responsibility can be practiced through the participation and the involvement of stakeholders in strategic decision-making. Responsibility to the stakeholders enables the company to follow market and society trends and to have a thorough knowledge of the changing values of stake holders. This can help companies to understand better their stakeholder's needs and to satisfy them efficiently.

Accountability : This principle is defined as the predisposition of an organisation to provide explanations and justifications for the actions of key stakeholders, impacted by its judgments, intentions, acts and omissions, if called upon to do so. Women Directors need to consider that, the central issue of accountability is determining the extent to which stakeholders have access to adequate, accurate, understandable, and up to date information, on the basis of which they can act. The concretisation of accountability allows the company to receive a better evaluation from outside and increases the stakeholder's confidence which can improve there liability, the credibility and the reputation of the company in its environment.

Fairness : Fairness has two different perspectives: protecting all the shareholders interests and ensuring equitable treatment of the stakeholders. In fact, the board must ensure the fairness in execution of contracts between the company and resource providers. Women Directors must understand clearly that practicing fairness in decision-making and in dealing with stakeholders can increase the satisfaction of the latter. The study of Herramann *et al.* (2001) showed that German customer perception of price fairness is positively correlated with their satisfaction suggest that empathy and the willingness of the company to treat fairly their stakeholders lead to the satisfaction of the latter.

Transparency : The company provides adequate disclosure and timely information to its stakeholders regarding its operations and activities. This information relate to the financial performance, corporate governance, the ownership structure, the voting rights, the directors profiles, the key executives and their remuneration the integrity of information and the timeliness of the communication are the key drivers of stakeholder's satisfaction. Disclosure is an important aspect in the sustainability of the relationship between the company and its stakeholders. Indeed, a study conducted in Germany by showed that stakeholders place a high value on the fact that the company does not hide anything and communicates openly about its financial condition and operations transparently.

Women Directors will find the following of relevance too -

- **Integrity**

The Board should lead the company to conduct its business in a fair and transparent manner that can withstand scrutiny by stakeholders.

- **Sustainability**

The Board should guide the business create value and allocate it fairly and sustainably for reinvestment and distribution among stakeholders, including shareholders, directors, employees and customers.

- **Leadership**

An effective Board should head each company. The Board should steer the company to meet its business purpose in both the short term and the long-term.

- **Capability**

The Board should have an appropriate mix of skills, experience and independence to enable its members to discharge their duties and responsibilities effectively.

For Women Directors the Pre-requisites of Good Corporate Governance would comprise -

- ***Tailored Legislation-*** *effective* legislation consisting of suitable, clear and crisp rules, regulations and principles is a much coveted pre-requisite for successful implementation of the concept of corporate governance.
- ***Independence of the Board-*** An independent board is the most essential constituent of good corporate governance. The Board members should have the ability to take decisions independently without any subservience to commercial dealings of the company and whims of the management.
- ***A skilful Board-*** The Board should be highly diverse and skilful. The members have to be handpicked and must possess the requisite technical expertise, legal and financial skills. The Board must also be well aware of the legal and regulatory requirements. A skilful board should fulfil the following requirements, at all times—
  - ***Board appointments*** need to be made carefully so that objective and goal-oriented people are selected.
  - ***Induction and training*** must be provided to board members at regular intervals. This would ensure quality and competence in the Board to achive the aganda.
  - ***Board meetings*** must be useful and should discuss a carefully planned agenda and strategies.
  - ***Board performance*** has to be meticulously monitored at regular intervals.

- ***An Audit Committee-*** A competent audit committee must be formed to ensure that internal and statutory audit is conducted in a fair and a transparent manner. It must also otherwise ascertain that policies/ regulations are complied with and key issues are reported to the board in a timely manner.
- ***Risk*** is an essential element that can affect the functioning of a company. Therefore, there should be effective means to identify and manage the involved risks. It is the responsibility of the Board to mitigate and deter these risk factors.

The prerequisites refer to the fulfilment of the pre-conditions on which depends the success of corporate governance. The success of the firm that complies with success of corporate governance prerequisites can reassure the stakeholders with regard to the protection of their interests. The presence of qualified, experienced and competent directors on corporate boards ensures the provision of expertise, knowledge and diligence required to run the business well and to develop the company resources. The existence of clear rules of corporate governance shows the companies commitment to ensure fairness and justice in its relationship with stakeholders.

The concept of corporate governance is rather complex. Various studies undertaken and research work conducted by Asian Development Bank, International Monetary Fund, Organisation for Economic Cooperation and Developments indicate that there can be no single model of good corporate governance. Different legal systems and a variety of needs across the globe have led to the development of a variety of approaches to corporate governance. Different economies follow tailored models of corporate governance. Anglo-Saxon, German, Japanese and Indian models of corporate governance are widely followed across the globe.

- **Anglo-American model:** This model is termed 'Anglo-Saxon model' and is used as the basis of corporate governance in USA, UK, Canada, Australia, and some commonwealth countries. The shareholders appoint directors who in turn appoint the managers to manage the business. Thus, there is separation of ownership and control. The board usually consist of executive directors and few independent directors. The board often has limited ownership stakes in the company. Moreover, a single individual holds both the position of CEO and chairman of the board. This model relies on effective communication between shareholders, board and management with all important decisions taken after getting approval of shareholders (by voting).

- **German model:** This is termed the two tier board model as there are two boards viz. the supervisory board and the management board. It is used in countries like Germany, Holland, France, etc. Usually a large majority of shareholders are banks and financial institutions. The shareholder can appoint only 50 per cent of members to constitute the supervisory board. The rest are appointed by employees and labour unions.
- **Japanese model:** This model is also called the business network model, usually shareholders are banks/financial institutions, large family shareholders, corporate with cross-shareholding. There is a supervisory board which is made up of board of directors and a president, who are jointly appointed by shareholder and banks/financial institutions. This is rejection of the Japanese 'keiretsu'- a form of cultural relationship among family controlled corporate and groups of complex interlocking business relationships, where cross-shareholding is common most of the directors are heads of different divisions of the company. Outside director or independent directors are rarely found on the board.

- **Indian model:** The model of corporate governances found in India is a mix of the Anglo-American and German models. This is because in India, there are three types of Corporation's viz. private companies, public companies and public sector undertakings (which includes statutory companies, government companies, banks and other kinds of financial institutions). Each of these corporations have a distinct pattern of share-holding. For example in case of companies, the promoter and his family have almost complete control over the company. They depend less on outside equity capital. Hence in private companies the German model of corporate governance is followed.

The Anglo-Saxon Model–Based on Enterpreneurship and Private Property

The Anglo-Saxon model is characterised by the dominance in the company of independent persons and individual share-holders. The manager is responsible to the Board of Directors and shareholders, the latter being especially interested in profitable activities and received dividends. It ensures the mobility of investments and their placement from the inefficient to the developed areas, there is lack of strategic development. In the US, financial markets activities dominate the allocation of ownership and control rights into organisations. Legislation always appeared hostile to concentration, especially in the banking industry, but in the recent years there have been new regulations forced by the new economic trends: the increasing influence of boards, Investors are increasingly demanding and cautious and managers give more importance to key business issues. Enterprises are required to disclose more information compared to those Japanese or German. On Stock Exchanges (NASDAQ) smaller companies are also present, even if some are still growing and developing. Corporate governance was encouraged by the work of associations which introduced a motion to support shareholders, such as National Association of Investors Corporation (founded in 1951) which advises on investments on the stock exchange and National Council of Individual Investors, which protects interests of the shareholders before regulatory authorities. Mainly considering transparency and access to information, strengthening the relationship between regulators and shareholders, and promoting business ethics.

The governance model is operative in organisations at three levels: Firstly of shareholders-Secondaly of directors-Thirdly of managers, since managers authority derives from the administrators. Legislation limits the rights of shareholders to intervene in the current activities of the entity, for example, they can only decide the elected members of the Board. However, they can influence changes in the managers' attitude and manner of leading; they may decide to liquidate holdings or refuse to increase capital contribution to the entity, thus stopping funding. The Securities and Exchange Commission (SEC) has reduced its strict rules on collective activities of shareholders, proposing regulations to encourage investment relationship that allows managers and owners to discuss possible advantages and disadvantages of business strategy. Institutional investors play an important role in Anglo-Saxon systems. They dominate the UK, holding even two-thirds of the equity of companies. Investment relationship – a feature of UK governance system– is gaining ground in the United States in relations between company management and institutional investors. There are critics who assert that the this is due to repeated failures of internal and external control mechanisms. The Anglo-Saxon countries are characterised by the emergence of financial markets and strong banking restrictions, especially regarding the holding of shares in companies outside the banking sector. Great Britain can be perceived as a special presence, recognising the importance of the financial market in London, where many national companies are listed. The banking system does not have a central role in governance structures, banks being considered merely credit providers. In the economic entities, capital structure is dispersed and shareholder power is stable compared with that of managers. The Governance model (similar to the American) is dominated by the influence of external capital markets, through merger and acquisitions, but also through the control exercised over securities trading. Regulatory institutions act to protect investors by implementing specific policies and practices of the corporate governance system. Such a system requires an independent Board, responsible for monitoring and control of management, to improve its organisational performance and recovery. In the UK, but also in other Anglo-Saxon countries, where the market economy has developed significantly through sustained economic growth, there is a high degree of dispersion of capital and shareholder structures. People can directly intervene for economic development by holding shares and inverting is the capital market.

For Promoting the Continental-European Model – Is characterised by Major Shareholders' Interests

The Continental European model is characterised by a high concentration of capital. Shareholders have common interests with the organisation and participate in management and control. Managers are responsible to a wider group of stakeholders, besides shareholders, such as unions, business partners, etc. In Italy, the idea of the corporation dates back to ancient Rome, from the time of Emperor Trajan. At that time their where institutions collegia artificum similar to the contemporary institutions, which were legal entities for various types of trade. The members of the collegia artificum enjoyed tax benefits. They were inspired by the example of Greek society and their goal was to assist entrepreneurs. Italian corporatism saw two levels: the Catholic and Fascist. Catholic-inspired corporatism appeared in 1891 and grew to the early-twentieth century. They are synonymous with Giuseppe Toniolo, economist and sociologist, who promoted solidarity, rejecting individualism and liberal doctrines. Fascist corporatism developed during the years 1920-1940, and its general principles were set out in the Charter of Labour in 1927 and were institutionalised with the advent of new corporations, bringing together different categories of entrepreneurs and workers. 1939 led to the crucial step of establisment of the Chamber Fascia. The 1980s brought to attention a new concept, later debated in Italian literature: neocorporatism. Currently, market and companies management regulation is prevalent in a less receptive environment and exposed to adverse conditions. Socio-economic reality generated different structures of distribution and control management, each specific to the reference market and with special characteristics. Ownership and control of listed companies is significantly concentrated, shareholders can intervene in the management process. In the German system of governance, the enterprise is seen as the combination of various interest groups coordinating national interest objectives. From a historical point of view, German banks have played an important role in corporate decisions. Only one of four companies in Germany is entitled to enter into public transactions, thus, most companies seek financial assistance from banks. Great importance is given to the protection of creditors, even to the point where a bank might dominate a firm. Unlike the USA, German banks can act only for their own clients. This ensures the depositary voting rights to control the decisions and votes in a company. In Germany, the corporate governance system is a dual one, national policy provides employees access to information and participation in various activities of the enterprise and industrial democracy. Within companies their is an executive board and a supervisory council. The first effectively manages the company, but under the direction of the second, most decisions are, necessarily, confirmed by it. Such a governance structure is a mechanism for Effective management monitoring and control.

The Japanese Model – Specific to a Oriented Control Governance System

The Japanese model brings, us anew, the holding concept, which designates industrial groups consisting of companies with common interests and similar strategies. The managers' responsibility manifests itself in relations with shareholders and keiretsu (a network of loyal suppliers and customers). Keiretsu represents a complex pattern of cooperation and also competition relationships, characterised by the adoption of defensive tactics in hostile takeovers, reducing the degree of opportunism of parties involved and keeping long-term business relationships. Most Japanese companies are affiliated with this group of trading partners. The characteristic pattern of governance is dominated by two types of legal relationships: one of co-determination between shareholders and unions, customers, suppliers, creditors, government and another ratio between administrators and those stakeholders, including managers. The necessity of the model results from the fact that the activity of a company should not be upset by the relations between all these people, relationships that generate risks. Management decisions pursue improving the income and power of an enterprise, in particular through specific corporate governance practices, although sometimes the shareholders control on the management can be hampered. Therefore, the Japanese model (similar to the German one) is based on internal control; it does not focus on the influence of strong capital markets, but on the existence of those strategic share-holders such as banks. As in Germany, major shareholders are actively involved in the management process, to stimulate economic efficiency and to penalise its absence. It is also aims to harmonise the interests of social partners and employees of the entity.

The Japanese governance system facilitates the monitoring and flexible financing of enterprises, effective communication between them and the banks, as the main source of financing comprises bank loans. It should be noted that the owners are other companies or banks, control management strategies; ownership is always oriented to control. Most packages are held by fixed shareholders who can also be major creditors, suppliers, customers, in order to maintain long-term relationships of trust and not only to obtain gain. In Japan, corporate policies are influenced by the active intervention of the government, since officials are stakeholders in many companies. The Central Bank and Ministry of Finance are monitoring the supervision and control within the company, in its relations with its strategic partners. Government structures have created an informal negotiation system to implement certain policies and corporate strategies (*gyosei shido*). In the 1980s, governmental influence manifested itself indirectly through appointments to the board of directors and managers of some functionaries out of system (*amakudari*). They retired at the age of 55 and belonged to various private companies to lead and participate effectively in developing strategies, driven by government policies. Corporate governance oriented to control is easily achieved in Japan due to concentrated shareholder structures, unlike the United States. Many voices say that Japan has to go the longest road to improve standards of governance, a significant gap noted now, as in the past, in the lack of corporate transparency. The existing situation is seen as a consequence of the market dominated by companies founded and ran by families. Banks and other institutional investors have usually a minor role in terms of corporate governance discipline. Their major responsibility is to provide debt financing, the existence of equity and bank directors should occupy top management positions. If an entity is profitable, bank's role can be limited to monitor and protect role can be the interests of foreign investors. At present, Japan's system is focused on transactional networks and not enough on individuals. Relations between keiretsu and stable banking systems are generally based on strong management and are sometimes even isolated. There are two favourable factors: the first refers to passivity of shareholders and second is the predominance of internal directors.

Convergences and Divergences of Different Systems Worldwide

The study on models of corporate governance in various

countries provides the image of the main specific features of Anglo-Saxon, Continental European, and Asian structures of Corporate governance Viewed in parallel, the features of those three models have important similarities and differences, as shown in the following table (Table 1.1).

Table 1.1 – The main features of corporate governance models

	Anglo-Saxon	**Continental Europe**	**Japanese**
Oriented towards Considers	stock market shareholders' property rights	banking market shareholders' property right and company's relationships with its employees	banking market stakeholders' interests (keiretsu)
Shareholding structure	dispersed	concentrated	concentrated (cross possession of shares)
Management	executive directors non-executive directors	Supervisor Board Board of Directors	Board of Directors
Control system	external	internal	internal
Accounting system	GAAP	IFRS	GAAP and IFRS

The Japanese system is difficult to understand for outsiders. From a historical perspective, it is based on legal recognition at national level of a mixture of public and private property, in which to each citizen is accepted the right to a fair share of all those things strictly necessary for the welfare. Power of property and rights of debts are equally divided between participants only theoretically. Although corporations in Japan resemble the structure of those of the United States, here the interest of shareholders overrides all else. Their status is clearly different in the two models. Models of governance in Germany and Japan are characterised by the strong presence of interested parties (stakeholders), especially banks, which increases the efficiency of corporate governance and provides competitive advantages in the two countries. In opposition, the populist policy of the United States inhibits the influence of such stakeholders, leading to inefficiency and increased agency costs. German and Japanese systems focus on expanding public-private partnership that leads to possible competitive advantage by reducing costs of risk capital.

Each model was developed based precisely on cultural, historical and technological features, and they show the way and means in which the models appeared under the influence of national economic and social specific conditions. It turned out that no model of governance is perfect and even better, their existence over time showing that each one is effective in its own way, and corporate governance structure specific to a country is difficult to transfer to another country.

Western societies have promoted corporate governance as a democratic culture, based on dynamism and willingness to impose on the market, which created the conditions of globalisation. Essential objectives are to obtain profit, support creativity, research and innovation, solutions to globalisation requirements. The new economy and knowledge based society place at the centre of corporate governance that form of capital which has become increasingly important – human capital. In some European countries (Belgium, Spain, Portugal, Italy etc.), but also at the international organisations level (OECD), the objective of developing mechanisms of governance is improving the information provided on the capital market and improve company performance, competitiveness and/or access to capital. For countries with tradition in the field and liquid capital markets (UK, France, Germany, etc.), the main objective of these mechanisms relates to the Board of Directors' work, meaning improve its quality and the quality of information about corporate governance. Good governance is still difficult to measure, organisations carrying out such assessments need more representative criteria so that entities must notify their management processes in an efficient manner. The implemented model essentially depends on the firm's theory of voluntary or mandatory approach, but also on the boundaries between markets, entrepreneurs and civil society. Corporate Governance is thus Governance by the Board and Woman have an important role to fulfill in leading, guiding and directing the affairs of the companies through effective Board led Corporate Governance. Corporate Governance has at its core the idea that the Company can govern the corporation. The group of people who direct the affairs of the corporation, its Directors must ensure that the Company works morally and its concerns are ethical. Human Capital Development and the encouragement and involvement of women is critical to this process of growth and development.

Chapter 2

Women Directors

The Sea Change in India with the SEBI Listing Mandating Women on Board

The SEBI guidelines are a little short of revolutionary as these ensure the presence of women on corporate Boards.

The recent SEBI guidelines have mandated that there must be women on a Board.This is to ensure that gender diversity becomes a reality and the gap between rhetoric and reality is bridged. SEBI has provided a legal framework to make sure that this happens.

Legal Framework-India

Companies Act, 2013

The New Companies Act, 2013 has been enacted to replace the old Companies Act of 1956, with the objective of bringing in more accountability and robust corporate governance. The second proviso to Section 149 of the Companies Act, 2013 provides that such class or classes of companies as may be prescribed shall have at least one woman director. Rule 3 of the Companies (Appointment and Qualification of Directors) Rules, 2014 provides that (i) every listed company, (ii) every other public company having paid up share capital of one hundred crore rupees or more; or turnover of three hundred crore rupees or more shall appoint at least one woman director.

[This landmark Act is considered by many to be the tipping point in India Inc's history, as it seeks to ensure adequate representation of women on the Board as well as to inculcate greater diversity of views across the boards of companies.

The Act mandating greater representation of women on boards is a path-breaking law in India Inc's history, especially since it marks a significant change in the way women are represented in senior leadership. However, for the Act to be a success, the onus of ensuring greater representation of women primarily rests on the board members.]

SEBI- Clause 49 of Listing Agreement

Clause 49 (II)(A)(1) of the Listing Agreement provides that the Board of Directors of the company shall have an optimum combination of executive and non-executive directors with at least one woman director and not less than fifty per cent of the board of Directors comprising non-executive directors. The provisions regarding appointment of woman director as provided in Clause 49 (II)(A)(1) has been made applicable with effect from April 01, 2015.

Current Scenario

Category	*Numbers*
Public Listed Companies	**1470**
Total Number of Independent Directors on Board	**8990**
Number of Women Independent Directors on Board	**350**
Current Women on Board percentage	**4 Per cent**
Vacancies to be filled	**966**
Deadline for filling up the position	**1st October, 2014**

Legal Mandate for Women on Boards of Companies- Global Scenario

[Norway is a clear forerunner by being the first develo-ped country to make it mandatory for approximately 500 state-owned and privately-owned businesses to have 40 per cent women representation on board, as early as in 2006. France and Italy followed Norway in 2010 and 2011 respectively with a 40 per cent reservation of women on boards.

While key developed countries have quotas for women representation in board or senior leadership, developing countries lack any formal mandate.

Countries like China have a relatively stronger woman representation on board compared to the other developing countries, but do not have a formal mandate.

India seems to be the forerunner in setting up such a mandate. If this Act proves to be effective, India may just be a leading example for the other developing nations.

We also have other developed countries such as the United States that have no quota for women represen-tation on board. However, what is interesting is despite no quota, the United States has 16 per cent women representation on boards and 14 per cent women representation at chief executive levels.]

Women's representation in top management

[The proportion of women sitting on corporate boards and executive committees in Asian companies is strikingly low compared with Europe and the United States, even though women remain under-represented in those regions too. On average, women account for six per cent of seats on corporate boards in the ten markets studied, and eight per cent of those on executive committees. The comparative figures in Europe and the United States are 17 per cent and 10 per cent, and 15 per cent and 14 per cent respectively. There are, however, significant differences between markets in Asia.

In India, the female labour participation rate is 35 per cent – one of the lowest in the world. China by contract has one of the world's highest female labour participation rates, at 64 per cent but still only eight per cent of corporate board members and nine per cent of executive committee members are women.

The narrow representation of women at the top of the corporate hierarchy is not the only problem. If more women are to reach senior positions, they have to be present in the pipeline that feeds these positions. In the West, female labour participation rates are reasonably high and women are well-represented in the work force overall.

In South Korea, a very small proportion of women move into middle management. A rare exception is Singapore, where, if women reach the senior manage-ment of a company, they appear to have a relatively good chance of joining its executive committee.

On issues relating to gender in boardrooms it is states that there is no settled view or agreement on the extent of the glass ceiling effect IE. The Lack (lack of a gender neutral Stated Process, appointment process), the existence of pay discrimination for female directors or the impact of gender diversity on corporate performance. In terms of equity, the board appointment process is found to display a gender bias in the case of non-executive directors. This is a gender bias in the sense that the probability of a boardroom appointment going to a woman is dependent on whether a woman has stepped down from the board in the recent period. The odds on making a female appointment at the non-executive level never high are significantly enhanced when a non-executive woman has stepped down in the prior period. The appointment process for non-executives is not gender neutral.

The absence of a clear connection between gender diversity and company performance does not undermine the case for greater levels of gender diversity in the boardroom.

Female representation at top management Levels brings informational and social diversity benefits to the top management team, enriches the behaviour exhibited by managers throughout the firm, and motivates women in middle management. The result should be improved managerial task performance and thus better firm performance. There is a slight to this Cavent.

Female representation in top management improves firm performance but only to the extent that a firm's strategy is focused on innovation, in which context the informational and social benefits of gender diversity and the behaviours associated with women in management are likely to be especially important for managerial task performance.

What is holding women back?

Top 5 barriers in Asia	*Top 5 barriers in Europe*
1. "Double burden" syndrome (women balancing work and domestic responsibilities)	1. "Double burden" syndrome (women balancing work and domestic responsibilities)
2. Absence of female role models	2. Women's reluctance to promote themselves
3. "Anytime, anywhere" performance model	3. Absence of female role models
4. **Lack of pro-family public policies or support services (e.g., child care)**	4. "Anytime, anywhere" performance model
5. Women's reluctance to promote themselves	5. Women's tendency to network less effectively than men

Country-wise variations of Women in Top Management

1. **India.** Gender gaps in basic literacy and in the numbers entering higher education mean that India has one of the lowest female labour participation rates in Asia, and the world. The fundamental issue is educational opportunity. Only about 30 per cent of the work force at junior level is female compared with 65 per cent in China. In addition, the notion that women must take care of the family is particularly strong. About 45 per cent of women's said this is what influences most or many senior women to leave the workplace in India.
2. **China.** Among Asian countries, China has one of the highest female labour participation rates, owing to the influence of the communist party. Women usually do not drop out of the work force when they have children

because childcare is relatively available and affordable. Women still face limitations in winning promotions and there is a significant falling-off in female representation at senior levels. Gender diversity is not yet a strategic imperative for Chinese companies, with the proportion of companies saying companies saying attainment of gender parity at board level was among their top ten priorities.

3. **Japan.** Traditional thinking has been that women should stay at home after marriage. Accordingly, about 60 per cent of married women quit or change their job. Although there are signs of improvement in terms of education and wages parity, gender stereotyping is still common in Japan and women themselves express lower levels of ambition to reach executive leve. Japan thus has one of the lowest levels of female representation on boards and executive committees in Asia.

4. **Australia.** Levels of female representation on boards and executive committees approach those in the United States and the United Kingdom. But this has not long been the case. It is only in the past few years that government and business have stepped up their efforts to broaden gender diversity, with impressive results. In 2010, the Sex Discrimination Commissioner recommended that the government set a target whereby 40 per cent of places on the boards of public companies should be filled by women. The Australian Stock Exchange soon responded by implementing a new listing rule requiring companies to set and report on gender diversity targets. In addition, the Male Champions of Change Group, which now includes 22 corporate and public service leaders, lobbies for female representation and helps shape best practice. The Australian Institute of Company Directors runs a mentoring programme for potential women board directors. And the Chief Executive Women

Organisation, a group of more than 200 leading businesswomen, continues to shape public debate and support the development of female talent. Although there is still scope for improvement, Australia is an example for Asia of how to make change happen.

Right skills of potential women board members

Mentoring and sponsorship programmes: 'Sponsorship' by existing board members is considered to be pivotal in providing female employees with the visibility to apply for board membership. Public mentoring and sponsorship programmes may be the primary and impactful sources of high quality talent.

List of qualified candidates: One key element is to have a list of qualified candidates and the panel suggested that a neutral body to maintain this list may be the most practical and State foreword approach. This list can be shared with organisations based on the requirements.

Quota allocation: There may be a need for radical measures such as quota allocation at each level to encourage participation across organisations.

Women employee retention mechanisms: Women employee retention and development programmes all the way up to the Board level could be interesting ways to not just have a higher representation of women at senior roles, but also on the board.

Coaching on developing networking skills: Another critical point is to invest in coaching women and helping them build on their networking skills.

Recommendations

1. Create and maintain a talent database.
2. Focus on traditional as well as alternate channels of sourcing.
3. Drive skill development through training, certifications and benchmarks.
4. Provide networking opportunities.

5. Address internal and external factors impacting gender diversity.

Public Sector Directorships occupied by Women in India

- Public sector Directorships occupied by women increased marginally from 15 in 1995 to 18 in 2007 but declined in percentage terms from 52 per cent of all women Directorships in 1995 to 27 per cent of the Directorships in 2007.
- The most prominent contributor to the Public Sector Directorships were the public sector banks. Out of the total of 206 Women Directorships provided by the public sector for the period 1995 to 2007, 98 Directorships or 48 per cent of the public sector women directorships were provided by the public sector banks. Public Sector Banks also accounted for 16 per cent of all women Directorships during 1995 to 2007.
- The numbers as well as percentages of Professional Women Directorships also show an increasing trend from 10 per cent of the Women Directorships in 1995 to 21 per cent in 2007.
- Women Directorships held by funding agencies and private sector banks in various corporate as well as on their Boards though showing an overall increasing trend also fluctuated. This could be possibly because of the ups and downs of the economy and the dependence of companies on support from Funding agencies or banks.
- Amongst all the companies ICICI Bank is the single largest contributor to Women Directorships. Taking into account Women Directors on its own Board and adding Directorships held by women from the Bank on various corporates, ICICI accounted for 13 per cent of all Women Directorships for the period 1995 to 2007. HDFC as well as HDFC Bank also has many women Directors on their Boards.

- Based on the number of Directorships held in different companies for the period 1995 to 2007, the 116 women who were Directors of some company or the other during this period, have been ranked in terms of importance.
- Directorships held by private sector banks and financial Institutions including their directorships in private companies showed up and down fluctuations during this period. From three Directorships or 10 per cent of the Directorships in 1995 the percentage of women Directors under this category increased to nine Directorships or 23 per cent in 2000. It then declined to 17 per cent by 2005 and has been growing from there to reach 21 per cent of the Directorships in 2007.
- Of the total of 114 Women Directorship positions held by funding institutions, 56 positions in companies were held by one bank – Private Sector Bank. In addition to these positions with private companies that come with financial support, Private Sector Bank also had on its own Board, Board positions were assigned to women for the period 1995 to 2007. Private Sector Bank Bank also had Board positions were assigned to women. ICICI alone accounts for 80 Women Directorships or 13 per cent of all women Directorships for the period 1995 to 2007. Private Sector Bank also account for a large number of women Directorships. These Directorships are however largely confined to the Boards of only these two companies and does not extend to other company Boards.
- As per (working papers No. 324 by IIM) Bangalore professors titled women power incorporate India women directorship on India corporate board 1995-2007 strength) by Chander Shekhar and Murali Dharan concluded after analysing data on women directors on the board of once 166 companies collected for period 1995-2007 that women directorship on corporate

boards show and increasing thread in numbers as well as in percentage terms from 29 or 1.66 of all directorships in 1995 to 67 or 3.63 of all directorship in 2007. These percentage are still much power than those of many industry advance countries for which such data is available.

Women in Public Sector Banks

- They have already smashed the glass ceiling in private sector banking in India. Now, Indian women are slowly but surely making their way to the top in public sector banks too. In the past year itself, five women have moved into the corner office at state-run banks in the country, joining a small club of women at the top of the banking industry across the world.
- Ms Usha Ananthasubramanian took over as Chair-person and Managing Director Punjab National Bank, soon after Ms Arundhati Bhattacharya became the top boss of State Bank of India, the largest bank in India while Ms Vijayalakshmi R. Iyer became the head of Bank of India and Ms Shubhalakshmi Panse became Chairman and Managing Director of Allahabad Bank. The policy of compulsory rural Bank Posting led several women to leave bank Jobs.
- Making it to the top is never easy for women in any field. But it's particularly hard in the public sector where women initially took up jobs to help support the family and held back from taking up more challenging roles. It took more than 30 years after bank nationalisation in 1969 for a woman to be appointed head of a state-run bank. Ms Ranjana Kumar became chairman and managing director of Indian Bank only in 2000.
- The numbers are still small, but have been gathering pace recently. Today, state-owned banks headed by women have a 45 per cent share of deposits and 50 per cent of advances of all public sector banks.

Boards are of three types

1. The Ceremonial Board
2. The Liberated Board
3. The Progressive Board

With women on Board we have to also ensure that they play progressive roles. This should not deteriorate to a Panchayati Raj like situation. There was a constitutional Article 74 amendment which mandated that the Panchayats should be empowered and women should head the Panchayats. These are base level organisations which discharge administrative functions at the village level and whose heads are elected members women did get elected to head the Panchayats as mandated, however, in several cases it was found that they continued to be ceremonial heads while men husbands, brothers, fathers uncle's father-in-laws still pulled all the strings and wielded all power. Thus, we should not have a ceremonial Board with wives, mothers and sisters, who are meant more to be seen and not heard on the Boards. If this happens in large measure it would defeat the spirit behind the SEBI guidelines. This taxonomy of Boards draws upon Ram Charan's categorisation which states that Boards began their evolution in the pre-Sarbanes-Oxley era of passivity. They were termed Ceremonial Boards as they existed because they were required to be created Chief Excutive Officers (CEO) still held sway in the Boardroom. The Boards performed a perfunctory role they echoed the CEO and rubber stamped all major decisions, there was generally a tight minute by minute agenda of these Boards a long drawn out presentation and all this frenetic activity precluded any discussion of the real issues engaging the Company. The Boards performed a compliance role and they were created to subserve just the ceremonial role. The Directors of these Boards also enjoyed a delicious measure of anonymity their names were rarely reported and in the golden era of the sixties and early seventies pre-Watergate the media was also not very active. The Directors were unlikely to be embroiled if the Company ran into trouble. All they were required to do was 'ritualistically' attend the Board meetings, make up the quorums and endorse the actions. Taken thus, they were quiescent members. This was followed by the age of the Liberated Board. Most Boards jettisoned the ceremonial tinge to the Boards with the passage of the Sarbanes Oxley Act and the Chief Executive Officer also felt impelled to encourage his board to contribute to the making of policy and was compelled to listen with respect and attention. Though this was indeed progress the liberated Board brings in its wake a stream of querulous directors who can tie the CEO down like Gulliver and Lilliputians seriously throw the meetings Off track here Women of steel can work wonders by gently but firmly getting discussions back on track and not allow the meeting to meander away to meaninglessness. The dramatic change came when scandals like Enron overwhelmed the workplace it was not just an ethical issue boards were compelled to act when shareholder and bond holder values evaporated. A Liberated Board does lead to a high functioning team but if the members play to their own strengths all the time it also becomes that much more difficult to achieve anything tangible. This leads to the third stage of the evolution of the Boards as Progressive Boards. These Boards really contribute to the growth of the Company as they preoccupy themselves with legacy issues work done and are governed by the sage belief that as Andy Grove founder, former CEO of Intel is quoted by Fortune magazine as saying, To ensure that the success of a Company is longer lasting than any CEOs reign, than any market opportunity, than any product cycle the librated board a Progressive board with women of still steering it quoted by Ram Charan p. 9. Women are more effective on the Liberated Board this board is defined by Ram Charan as one which is uniformly effective as a team which still maintains an independent view-point. All directors contribute to a coherent dialogue that has lively debates, sticks to key issues, while dropping tangents and eventually leads to consensus and closure the Board and the CEO build a constructive and collaborative working relationship. This may seem platitudinous but women are generally better and more effective in creating such a Board where hard issues are confronted, not swept under the carpet and work proceeds in a spirit of collaboration.

The major changes to clause 49 of the Listing Agreement

- **Independent Directors:-** one-third to half depending whether the chairman of the board is a non-executive or executive position.
- **Non-Executive Directors:-**The total term of office of non-executive directors is now limited to three terms of three years each.
- **Board of Directors:-**The board is required to frame a code of conduct for all board members and senior management and each of them have to annually affirm compliance with the code.
- **Audit Committee:-** Financial statements and the draft audit report of management discussion and analysis of...
  - Financial condition
  - Result of operations of compliance with laws
  - Risk management letters
  - Letters of weaknesses in internal controls issued by statutory auditors
  - Internal auditors

  - Removal and terms of remuneration of the chief internal auditor
- **Whistle blower Policy:-**This policy has to be communicated to all employees and whistle blowers should be protected from unfair treatment and termination.
- **Subsidiary Companies:-**Fifty per cent non-executive directors and half and half independent directors depending on whether the chairman is non-executive or executive.

There is still a long way to go - No Woman Director in 56 NSE Listed Companies

As many as 56 companies including Tata Power, Alstom India, state-run ONGC and GAIL have failed to comply with regulator Sebi's norms to appoint at least one woman director on board, leading data provider Prime Database said. These non-compliant firms include a host of PSU (Public Sector Units) and PSBs (Public Sector Banks). All listed firms were required to have at least one woman director on their boards from April 1, 2015, as per a Sebi directive, as also under the Companies Act, 2013.

These rules are aimed at ensuring gender diversity in boardrooms. According to Prime Database, a total of 56 NSE-listed companies have not appointed a woman director on board. BEML, BPCL, Hindustan Organic Chemicals, HMT, IOC, MMTC, National Fertilisers, Power Finance Corp, Syndicate Bank, Rural Electrification Corp, Oriental Bank of Commerce, State Trading Corp and Madras Fertilisers are among the PSUs that are yet to comply with Sebi's directive. Some of the private entities that still have to induct women directors are Lanco Infratech, DB Corp, Valecha Engineering, Servalakshmi Paper and Salora International.

The rule was first announced by Sebi in February 2014 with an initial deadline of October 1 the same year that was later extended by six months. Since then, most of the companies listed on the national stock exchange (NSE) have hired a woman member on board. Interestingly, a significant number of firms appointed a woman member from the promoter family to comply with the rule within the deadline. Acting against listed firms without a mandatory woman director, Sebi in April 2015 announced a minimum Rs 50,000 fine and warned of further action, including against promoters and directors, if they remain non-compliant beyond six months.

The Securities and Exchange Board of India (SEBI) announced a four-stage penalty structure wherein fines would increase with the passage of time. The market watchdog had asked the stock exchanges to levy the fines as the violation relates to the Listing Agreement. The listed companies complying between April 1, and June 30, 2015 will have to pay Rs 50,000. Those complying between July 1 and September 30 would need to pay Rs 50,000 and an additional Rs 1,000 per day till compliance.

The listed firms complying on or after October 1, 2015 will have to pay Rs 1,42 lakh, plus Rs 5,000 per day till the date of compliance. For any non-compliance beyond September 30, 2015, the regulator may take any other action against the non-compliant entities, their promoters and/or directors or issue such directions in accordance with law, as considered appropriate.

Conclusion

- As Indian companies compete globally for access to capital markets, many are finding that the ability to benchmark against world-class organisations is essential.
- For a long time, India was a managed, protected economy with the corporate sector operating in an insular fashion.
- But as restrictions have eased, Indian corporations are emerging on the world stage and discovering that the old ways of doing business are no longer sufficient in such a fast-paced global environment.

Chapter 3

Ethics in Business

What is meant by ethics in business the moral compass, the code which determines what is right in business. In the Latin maxim Que custodiet ipso custodies the question posed is who will guard the Guards? Established values and principles a company uses to inform and conduct its activities. It should permeate a company's culture and drive its strategy, business goals, policies and activities. Usually found in a code of ethics. Business ethics is defined as the study of proper business policies and practices regarding potentially controversial issues, such as corporate governance, insider trading, bribery, discrimination, corporate social responsibility and fiduciary responsibilities. Business ethics are often guided by law, while other times at these provide a basic framework that businesses may choose to follow in order to gain public acceptance, Business ethics are principles and standards that determine acceptable conduct in business. Business ethics embraces the concept of social responsibility which is the responsibility of the business to maximise its positive impact and to minimise its negative impact on society. Laws and regulations encourage businesses to conform to the norms and laws of society. The Sarbanes Oxley Act brought these issues to the fore of Accounting Fraud, Misleading advertisement, unfair competitive practices internet theft. Ethical conduct helps to build trust, inspire confidence and validate relationships an identifiable

problem, situation, or opportunity that requires a person to choose from among several actions that may be evaluated as right or wrong, ethical or unethical.

How to Judge the Ethics of a Situation

Women can do this better then men as they have the reflexivity to check the situation from their stakeholders' position, including customers and competitors.

Many business issues may seem straightforward and easy to resolve on the surface, but are in reality very complex many things can prompt unethical behaviour:

1. Illustratively Overly aggressive financial or business objectives.
2. Abusive and intimidating behaviour
3. The Presence of Conflict of interest
4. Absented Fairness and honesty
5. Unclear Communications
6. Collusive Business relationships

    1. The most common ethical issue identified by employees.
    2. Advance personal interests over others' interests.
    3. Benefit self at the expense of the company.

Fairness and Honesty – the Heart of Business Ethics

- How employees use resources
- No harm to customers

- Accurate representations
- Disclosure
- False/misleading advertising
- Deceptive personal selling tactics
- Product safety and quality
- Unsubstantiated claims
- Product labelling

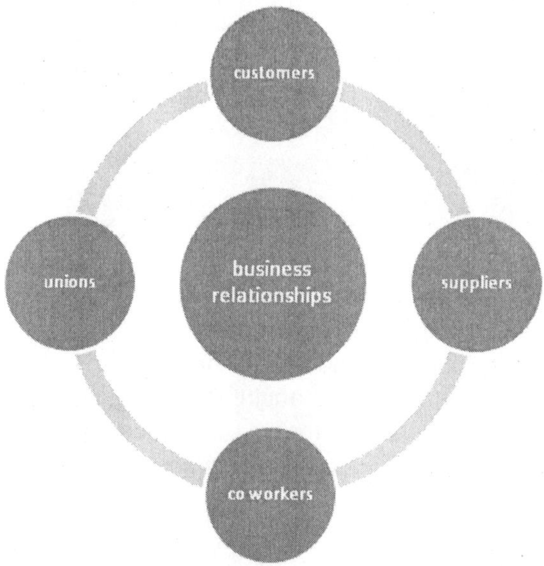

In business relationships with Suppliers Co workers, Unions, and Customers the level of honesty is Importent *Open discussion of ethical issues does not eliminate ethical problems; it does promote trust and learning in an organisation.* As also transparency which must be maintained do not ever deal in lies. These can be improved if there is a ***Codes of Ethics*** –

Formalised rules and standards that describe what a company expects of its employees *organisations with written standards of conduct are more likely to report misconduct when they observe it.*

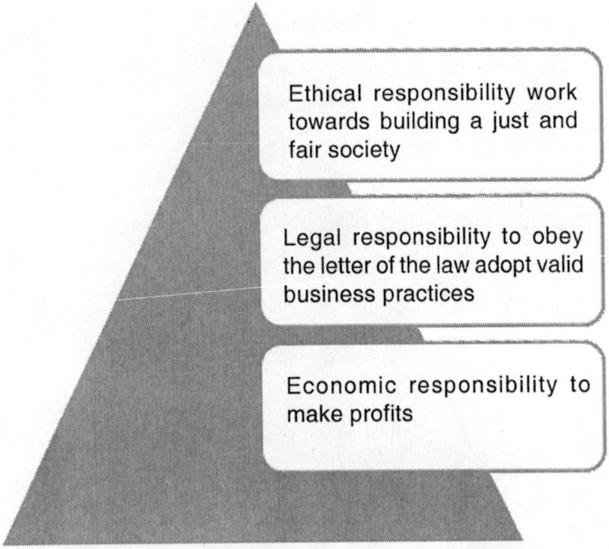

Whistle blower Protection is extended through such a code The act of an employee exposing an employer's wrongdoing to outsiders, such as the media or government regulatory agencies. Ethical business environment implies the extent to which businesses meet the legal, ethical, economic, and voluntary responsibilities placed on them by their stakeholders.

1. Economic
2. Legal
3. Ethical

Voluntary (philanthropic) are the corporate social responsibilities whereby the Board empowers the company to work in the best interests of the company and also to give back to society. **Is the Business of Business just Business?**

Milton Friedman had a view that corporate executives responsibility generally will be to make as much money as possible while conforming to the basic rules of the society both those embodied in law and those embodied in ethical custom.

The objective is the maximisation of consumption and production. The business of business is just business. This is not a maxim one can concur with if you consider the Business of Companies historically has embraced colonialism and slavery! So the element of ethics must always underlie both business personal and organisational conduct.

Formal Codes of Ethics

While many of the governance issues that organisations face are not new, the environment in which they confront them is more challenging than ever. Many companies are adopting legal compliance mechanisms which address ethics or conduct issues in formal documents.

Ethics @ Work

Some organisations have adopted a code of ethics for themself. Why?

- To define acceptable behaviour.
- To promote high standards of practice.
- To provide a benchmark for self-evaluation.
- To establish a framework for professional behaviour and responsibilities.
- As a vehicle for occupational identity.
- As a mark of occupational maturity they have formulated a clear.
- Written code of ethics which requires as a Sinquanon.
- Employee commitment.
- Employee training.
- Discipline process.
- Full disclosure.
- Builds expectations.
- A Resolution process – for effective conflict management. A formal code of business conduct and ethics This code of ethicsis. To be signed and adhered

to by employees and action can be taken against any employee for violation thereof.

Some organisations also have ethics officers but in the ultimate analysis, the foundations of ethical behaviour go well beyond corporate culture and policies these are rooted in one's moral training, lessons Parents and School teachers have taught from early childhood and which affect not just individual behaviour the competitive business environment and indeed society as a whole.

From an ethical dimension, at a fundamental level, the key issues of corporate governance involve questions concerning relationships and building trust both within and outside the organisation. Ethics is derived from the Greek word *Ethos* and embraces both work ethics and mores the conduct and culture of the organisation.

Business ethics reflects the philosophy of business, of which one aim is to determine the fundamental purposes of a company. If a company's purpose is to maximise shareholder returns, then sacrificing profits to other concerns is a violation of its fiduciary responsibility. Corporate entities are legally considered as persons in USA and in most nations. The 'corporate persons' are legally entitled to the rights and liabilities due to citizens as persons.

Ethics are the rules or standards that govern our decisions on a daily basis. Many equate ethics with conscience or a simplistic sense of right and wrong. Others would say that ethics is an internal code that governs an individual's conduct, ingrained into each person by family, faith, tradition, community, laws, and personal mores. Corporations and professional organisations, particularly licensing boards, generally will have a written Code of Ethics that governs standards of professional conduct expected of all in the field. It is important to note that law and ethics are not synonymous, nor are the legal and ethical courses of action in a given situation necessarily the same. Statutes and regulations passed by legislative bodies and administrative boards set forth the law. Slavery once was legal in the US, but one certainly wouldn't say forcibly enslaving humans can be consider to have been an ethical act.

Economist Milton Friedman writes that corporate executives' responsibility... generally will be to make as much money as possible while conforming to the basic rules of the society, both those embodied in law and those embodied in ethical custom. Friedman also said, the only entities who can have responsibilities are individuals...A business cannot have responsibilities. So the question is, do corporate executives, provided they stay within the law, have responsibilities in their business activities other than to make as much money for their stockholders as possible? And the answer to that is, no, they do not. A multi-country 2011 survey found support for this view among the informed public ranging from 30 to 80 per cent. Ronald Duska views Friedman's argument as consequentialist rather than pragmatic, implying that unrestrained corporate freedom would benefit the most in the long term. Similarly, author business consultant Peter Drucker observed, There is neither a separate ethics of business nor is one needed, implying that standards of personal ethics cover all business situations. However, Peter Drucker in another instance observed that the ultimate responsibility of company directors is not to harm—*primum non nocere.* Another view of business is that it must exhibit corporate social responsibility (CSR): an umbrella term indicating that an ethical business must act as a responsible citizen of the communities in which it operates even at the cost of profits or other goals. In the US and most other nations corporate entities are legally treated as persons in some respects. For example, they can hold title to property, sue and be sued and are subject to taxation, although their free speech rights are limited. This can be interpreted to imply that they have independent ethical responsibilities. Duska argues that stakeholders have the right to expect a business to be ethical; if business has no ethical obligations, other institutions could make the same claim which would be counterproductive to the corporation.

Ethical issues include the rights and duties between a company and its employees, suppliers, customers and neighbours, its fiduciary responsibility to its shareholders. Issues concerning relations between different companies include hostile take-overs and industrial espionage. Related issues include corporate governance; corporate social entrepreneurship; political contributions; legal issues such as the ethical debate over introducing a crime of corporate manslaughter; and the marketing of corporations' ethics policies. The three major areas of public concern regarding business ethics are executive pay, corporate tax avoidance and bribery and corruption.

Women passage strong moral campus, principle and values and are their for best sited to guide corporation and capability steer them in the Right Direction.

Chapter 4

Understanding the Concept of Sustainability

Women on Company Boards have an important role to play on sensitising the Company to the needs of the environment. The work of the Company should not be one which depletes resources or harms the environment. Preservation of the environment for sustainability and for future generation is a moral imperative that should guide the actions of the company. The High Level Panel on Global Sustainability led by the UN Secretary General has observed that by 2030 the world will need 50 per cent more food, 45 per cent more energy, 30 per cent more water. The challenges to eradicate poverty, reduce inequality, make growth inclusive and production and consumption more sustainable, while computing climate change and respecting all other planetary boundaries.

The most commonly accepted definition of sustainability is from the Brundtland Report for the World Commission on Environment and Development 1987 which defines it as: 'development that meets the needs of the present without compromising the ability of future generations to meet their own needs.' Sustainability recognises stakeholder rights i.e. the rights of interested parties e.g. employees, the community, suppliers, customers etc. Encourage co-operation between the company and its stakeholders in creating wealth, jobs and economic stability. Most basic definitions of innovation suggest that it is change or novelty induced by human creativity and necessitated by human requirements. Innovation is the result of interaction between individuals, organisations, systems and institutions using various signals like price, convenience and creativity to find the direction. It is the result of both individual actions and interactions with environments such as markets, organisations, systems or institutions. Scale of innovation may, however, differ. Thus, we have innovations that revolutionise the system as a whole, as also those that alter it only marginally. System-changing innovation goes beyond technological innovation, and includes organisational innovation as well. In all its myriad forms, innovation becomes a tool for development.

Women Directors better understand that development is a highly dynamic process that ensures economic growth and improvement in human indices. It becomes sustainable if it allows inter-generational replication and the results of the same are best suited to the environment. Thus, sustainable development meets the needs of the present without compromising the ability of future generations to meet their own needs. Sustainable development has its roots in the ideas of conservation of natural resources and protecting the environment. Thus, innovation, development and sustainability are not only conceptually close but almost inseparable in connotation.

The main challenge forewomen Director towards the transition to greener, cleaner and more equitable economic growth is to address the innovation issue not only from an economic, but also from a social and environmental dimension, which has also policy and governance implications. Innovation to be socially, environmentally and economically sustainable requires optimum developments on all these fronts together. The integration of sustainability into innovation polices is, thus, not an easy task. To achieve this, we need to integrate the evolutionary approaches into sustainable innovation policies by addressing environmental and social concerns.

Environmentally oriented innovations, also known as eco-innovations, bring the sustainable development realms of economy and environment into play, and also have an inherent effect on the social part of sustainable development. For centuries, the concept of innovation has been primarily related to economic issues, but environmental and societal pressures have spurred the rethinking of innovations in the context of sustainable development. As innovations are regarded as a means towards the transition from a traditional to a progressive society, an integrated perspective between social, economic and environmental dimensions needs our attention today. A significant obstacle to achieving sustainable development globally is the lack of a coherent approach that fully integrates all three pillars of sustainable development, i.e., social, economic and environmental perspectives, in pursuit of an over-arching goal. With our growing consciousness about the future, innovations have been directed towards sustaining our future resources for posterity. With this all-encompassing goal, it has become incumbent on all of us to direct innovation efforts towards future sustenance by reorienting our focus on environmental issues.

To begin with, companies need to address the environmental issues by formulating a robust Green Policy. The core objective of such a policy is to sustain the environment and conserve energy, water and other non-renewable resources by actively promoting the concepts of reduction, reuse and recycling, as also to maximise harnessing of renewable natural resources. The policy should aim to reduce consumption of natural resources like energy and water as also to minimise wastage by evaluating the existing operations and processes to ensure that they are as efficient as possible. In order to achieve this, reuse of the natural resources like wood, water, etc. to the maximum possible extent needs to be encouraged. Actively promoting procurement and use of recycled and eco-friendly material will help in sustaining the use of such precious materials for future use. Innovation process needs to be effectively dovetailed to the overall policy of environmental conservation so as to derive the best results. Harnessing solar energy, wind energy and rain water harvesting are a few examples of innovative ideas, which can help us achieve sustainable development in an environment-friendly way. For renewable resources (e.g. forests, water) and sinks for wastes (e.g. the atmosphere) to be used at sustainable levels, the rate of harvesting them (or discharge of emissions) must not exceed their rate of regeneration (or assimilative capacity). Non-renewable natural resources such as minerals do not regenerate on their own and in their case, sustainability becomes a question of maintaining utility over time, either by expanding reserves (through recycling, efficiency gains, exploration), or by investing income surpluses in alternative resources that will be available for future generations. Here the quality of sustainability assumes great significance. In such circumstances, inspite of our commitment to sustainable development, we are faced with the choice of weak sustainability, where it substitutes natural capital with human, or human-made capital (e.g. it depletes half of its primary forests to build factories, tourist resorts and schools); or strong sustainability, where it does not substitute natural capital with other forms but conserves the original resources by restricting its exploitation (e.g. conservation of a permanent estate of primary forest). It is in this context, the role of governance and policy intervention assumes a great significance.

As we all know, formulating a policy by itself would not guarantee its successful implementation. For this, we need to have a governance structure conducive to the environment. Globally, there is an increasing recognition that technocratic approaches have limitations, especially when it comes to solving complex problems that span numerous administrative boundaries and fragmented institutions. Where policy problems exceed a certain level of complexity and significance, and where existing institutions are too weak to manage these problems, governance initiatives emerge to produce solutions that are more beneficial. Women Director clearly no that to achieve this, the apparently independent units of power need to be interconnected through an efficient networking system. Women need to break down institutional silos and create horizontal channels for knowledge exchange and collaboration. By integrating distributed capacities for collective problem solving, governance networks allow diverse actors to work collaboratively towards mutually beneficial outcomes. However, only with an adequate level of social capital can a governance network create shared value and engage in processes of reflexive governance.

Woman no that sustainable development can be interpreted in many different ways, but at its core is an approach to development that looks to balance different, and often competing, needs against an awareness of the environmental, social and economic limitations we face as a society. The focus of sustainable development is far broader than just the environment. It's also about ensuring a strong, healthy and just society. This means meeting the diverse needs of all people in existing and future communities, promoting personal wellbeing, social cohesion and inclusion, and creating equal opportunity. The satisfaction of human needs and aspirations is the major objective of development. Human advancement in turn, depends on an on-going exchange between people and institutions. The decisions we make about how the world should be and how it can be improved depend on interactions among individual citizens, businesses, civil society and governments. These four categories function together in the complex and sometimes chaotic process of decision-making that we call politics. The term civil society is one we hear a great deal today, one which like sustainable development can be hard to pin down to an exact definition on which everyone agrees. The London School of Economics Centre for Civil Society defines it as the arena of un-coerced collective action around shared interests, purposes and values. The groups, associations and movements that make up civil society have played a part in all the important societal changes in the past century or more. Civil society organisations can be dedicated to specific issues or more general struggles. Indeed, they have been key to the success of very significant advances including universal suffrage, environmental protection, workers' rights and combating racial discrimination. Sustainable development is no exception and civil society organisations can leave a strong imprint in this direction.

Re-orientation of technology to suit the needs of a specific society where the same will be used holds the key to the success of innovation. The technologies of industrial countries are not always suited or easily adaptable to the socio-economic and environmental conditions of developing countries. To compound the problem, the bulk of world research and development addresses few of the pressing issues facing these countries. Not enough is done to adapt recent innovations in materials technology, energy conservation, information technology, and biotechnology to the needs of developing countries. These gaps must be covered by enhancing research, design, development, and extension capabilities. Otherwise, we come across a phenomenon known as uneven and insufficient innovation, which cannot support sustainable development.

This pattern of uneven and insufficient innovation is due in part to several distinct dynamics. First, many technologies provide positive externalities that transcend the control of firms or individual nation states, and are therefore subject to free-rider problems that lead to under-production by both markets and national innovation systems. Second, in comparison to industrialised countries, developing countries tend to offer smaller market incentives to private inventors and have weaker national innovation systems to encourage domestic invention, leading to fewer or poorly-adapted technologies for use in such countries. Third, incentive systems for innovation can reward inventors, but at the cost of end-user access—for example, high prices for inventions can impede access for the populations most in need of new technologies, such as medicines, off-grid energy supply or water purification devices.

Addressing these problems requires effective institutional arrangements at local, national and global levels. In recent years, these challenges of harnessing technological innovation for sustainable development have begun to be addressed through a variety of interventions in the global innovation system. Examples include financing arrangements, networks of scientific researchers, priority-setting processes, measures to facilitate sustained use and widespread access to a technology, international aid and trade agreements, and feedback loops connecting end-users and inventors/adapters. In general, these interventions have altered the rules, norms, resources or organisational configurations that shape the behaviour of major actors, including governments, private firms, researchers and end-users.

Here, it may be interesting to share the experience of the Indian Banking Industry in relation to the innovations in technology and processes and how it is helping in changing the face of banking in India. Over the years, the banking sector in India has seen a number of changes. Most of the banks have begun to take an innovative approach towards banking with the objective of creating more value for customers, and consequently, the banks. The use of information technology in the Indian banking sector was a corollary of the liberalisation process initiated in the country in the early 1990s. In spite of the initial scepticism, the technological innovations proved to be very useful to the population at large, thereby sustaining their popularity. Today we cannot imagine a world without debit cards, credit cards, mobile banking or on-line banking. Similarly, the innovations in the delivery process have helped the Indian Banking Industry to bridge the urban-rural gap. With a majority of the Indian population living in rural areas, rural banking forms a vital component of the Indian banking system. Besides, rural banking operations in India are rather different from urban operations, due to the strong disparity that exists between urban and rural life, and the needs of these two sections of people. Here the innovative processes leveraging on appropriate technology has helped change the face of banking in India, which is no longer elitist in nature. Banking correspondents with hand held devices offering banking services are a regular sight in the villages today. The success in opening huge number of accounts under the Pradhan Mantri Jan Dhan Yojana in a short span was possible because we could take the banks to the doorsteps of our citizens. This kind of doorstep banking no longer requires the customers to travel to the branches, nor does it require paper- based instruments for transaction – which not only ensures convenience for the society as a whole, but also immensely contributes towards a healthier environment. Thus, it is not out of place to suggest that innovation has helped us to dream about sustainable development in the field of banking with an ultimate aim of serving the society and environment.

Development efforts on various fronts now increasingly aim at fostering inclusive growth. None of us can deny that development efforts lack relevance and sustainability unless the spin-offs effectively touch the lives of the disadvantaged section of the society. In this context, the role of inclusive innovation in promoting sustainable development cannot be emphasised more. With the rapid growth of emerging economies, disparities have also increased in these countries. According to Kurt Larsen, a senior education specialist with World Bank Institute, Inclusive innovation is about utilising innovation to serve the needs of people at the economic base of the pyramid giving them access to basic goods, services and livelihood opportunities. It is inclusive innovation, which helps in maintaining balance and social stability, helps in redeployment of resources more effectively to ensure recoupling of growth thus paving the way for sustainable development. As a result, there is burgeoning interest by a variety of parties in the inclusive innovation agenda. It is, no doubt, a very positive development, which needs to be welcomed and encouraged. Research, interaction and exchange of information on the subject will actively contribute to the cause. UNCTAD estimates that achievement of the Sustainable Development Goal (SDG) requires US $ 5-7 trillion annually over the next 15 years. Efforts that are inclusive and environment friendly stand to benefit women most and also allow them to contribute to the GDP and to the economic growth indeed to India's economic resurgence. Advances in computing technology for instance allow women to work from home. This enables them to better manage dual fronts of home (where the presence of children requires their physical presence) and office which requires their mental energies. Computing part also offsets a perceived disadvantage of women in mathematical ability. Conceptually women are strong and they can target computing to it, math for them. Thus innovation benefits women. Women on corporate boards must take definite position to ensure that there is a cleaner production. Ensuring that corporates embraces green energy, agree to reduce the carbon footprint, allow the manufacturer and service providers to ensure that energy efficient technologies are adopted which lead to lesser waste, lesser affluence and have a positive impact on the environment ensuring greater sustainability. Building assets such as buildings, energy, transparent water and waste green financing is thus necessary component of sustainable development which women in their role as corporate directors must work to ensure that an ethical and...........responsible boards guides of business undertakings.

Chapter 5

The Glass Ceiling Shattering it to Smithereens

Glass can be smashed if one strikes it long enough or hard enough diamond is needed to cut through glass. Thus, women can polish their skills, increase their knowledge base and strengthen themselves through constant and continuous application, as a lifelong process to cut through the glass ceiling. The Glass ceiling is transparent one can see through it but it is nevertheless there. It exists as an unacknowledged discriminatory barrier that prevents women from rising to the top within an organisation. The Glass ceiling embodies invisible, culturally embedded assumptions and beliefs about the skills or competence of women that prevent them from reaching top management positions. These barriers restrain women and consequently limit organisations from attaining their full potential. It is not an Asian but a global construct even in America the Apple Pie mom the homemaker is prized and not the gutsy ambitious women who wants to ascend to the top of the slippery corporate ladder with her brains and because she can. She does not need today to disguise her feminity or to transcend it, or to use it. She should go up just as effortlessly as a man does using her innate professional skills, capabilities and confidence. Have the guts to hang in there have the guts to elbow out the big boys club Dare to lead have the audacity to flaunt your skills use your brute professional competence to touch the sky.

On 3rd April 2015 the Wall Street Journal filed the report quoted below:

Ellen Pao may have lost her gender-discrimination lawsuit against her former employer, the Silicon Valley venture-capital firm Kleiner Perkins Caufield & Byers, but the coverage of her case thrust a powerful metaphor back into the spotlight: the glass ceiling. Ellen Pao filed a high profile gender discrimination lawsuit against venture capital firm Kleiner Perkins, Caufield and Byers in San Francisco, Calif., in March. Ellen Pao by all accounts a highly qualified attorney with an outstanding track record of performance was passed over for promotion for the oldest of reasons known to womankind gender bias she butted her head against the glass ceiling. Oh the illusion of equality as the Wall street Journal wrote WSJ laments.

The term, the Glass Ceilings is used to describe the barriers faced by women and members of minority groups as they try to climb workplace ladders, may only grow more familiar in the tech world. In San Francisco Superior Court, Twitter faces a gender-bias suit from a former employee who claims that the company creates a glass ceiling for women that cannot be explained or justified by any reasonable business purpose. Twitter denies accusations in the suit. As for Ms Pao, she could appeal her case. The aftermath of this case will mean that many employers will improve their human resources practices, including creating more objective measures of success in performance reviews — a glaring issue in the Pao case — and will otherwise do everything in their power to avoid a public jury trial.

The glass ceiling first came to wide attention in March 1986, when The Wall Street Journal ran a special report by Carol Hymowitz and Timothy D. Schellhardt with that title. They detailed imperceptible obstacles faced by female managers, stymied by corporate tradition and prejudice rather than overt discrimination. The article popularised a term that had only been in print for two years. In March 1984, an article in Adweek quoted Gay Bryant, who at the time was leaving her position as editor of Working Woman magazine to become editor of Family Circle.

Women have reached a certain point—I call it the glass ceiling, Ms Bryant told Adweek. They're in the top of middle management, and they're stopping and getting stuck.

That same year, Ms Bryant used the phrase in a book that she edited, The Working Woman Report: Succeeding in Business in the '80s. In a 2009 interview, she said that she wasn't sure where the term came from, adding that she might have picked it up from one of the women she interviewed while researching the book.

Glass ceiling may, in fact, have originated five years earlier, growing out of a discussion between two women working at Hewlett-Packard. Katherine Lawrence, now chief operating officer and co-founder of the Colorado-based creative engineering firm Pingv, was one of those women. As she explained, she was working in 1979 for H-P's medical electronics division in Waltham, Mass. Over dinner with Maryanne Schreiber, a colleague there, Ms Lawrence noted that women at the company seemed able to rise only so far as managers before facing an unseen barrier. They hit this ceiling. This ceiling is invisible—a glass ceiling, she recalls telling Ms Schreiber.

A little later, in July 1979, Ms Lawrence spoke at the annual conference of the Women's Institute for the Freedom of the Press. I presented the concept of how in corporate America, the official policy is one way—the sky's the limit—but in actuality, the sky had a glass ceiling for women, she said.

Whatever be the origins of the form, however in it started, the success of the phrase glass ceiling is indisputable, spawning many variations, such as bamboo ceiling (for Asian-Americans), celluloid ceiling (for women in Hollywood) and marble ceiling (for women in government). As a figure of speech, at least, the glass ceiling seems to be reaching new heights.

In 1991, the US Department of Labor defined glass ceiling as those artificial barriers based on attitudinal or organisational bias that prevent qualified individuals from advancing upward in their organisation into management-level positions. The department's **Glass Ceiling Commission** (1991-1996) studied these barriers not only as they apply to women, but as they apply to minorities as well.

Women in Senior Management 1981, 1991, 2001, 2011 and 2015

Women in Management: Closer to breaking through the glass ceiling? Linda Wirth in Women, Gender & Work (ILO, 2001 ed. Martha Fetherolf Loutfi. *Women have made enormous progress in many countries in obtaining a greater share of professional and management jobs. The data show the significant role played by education and the growing diversification of women's careers. Nevertheless, research findings demonstrate how unbreakable the glass ceiling is. Women's overall share of management jobs rarely exceeds 20 per cent in most countries, yet they represent >40 per cent of the world's labour force. The higher the position the more glaring the gap between men and women. It is suggested that some career-building strategies and enterprise policies can help to speed up women's advancement to the top jobs although women are often better educated and qualified than men in the same job, women still find it difficult to reach top positions. They had to work harder and perform better than men to move ahead. Studies: In Jamaica, women had more years of schooling before joining labour force than men, advanced more quickly than men at middle management level but took significantly longer to achieve top level management positions. Turkish Civil Service –women progress in overall managerial jobs but get stuck at middle menegement level.* ***What is a real and practical constraint for women to achieve high level positions?***

1. Disproportionate responsibility –family, raising children, household tasks. Professional/managerial jobs often require long hours of recognition and eventual promotion.
2. Career progression structures and policies are around the ages of 30-40 as most important for career development which is the most intensive years for child rearing. Women who want both career and family must juggle heavy responsibilities in both domains. Women without family are often seen as potential mothers, thus even with education and training; they are often given less attention than their male counterparts.
3. Women in developing countries may have fewer difficulties obtaining management jobs due to
   (a) smaller proportion of the population attain higher education, so the skills and knowledge of qualified women are much in demand.
   (b) Extended family/inexpensive domestic help provide crucial support for childcare and household maintenance. Their is a lack of family-friendly workplace policies and limited opportunities for advancement to decision-making positions.

The general-case glass ceiling hypothesis states that not only is it more difficult for women than for men to be promoted up levels of authority hierarchies within workplaces but also that the obstacles women face relative to men become greater as they move up the hierarchy. Gender-based discrimination in promotions is not simply present across levels of hierarchy but is more intense at higher levels. Empirically, this implies that the relative rates of women being promoted to higher levels compared to men should decline with the level of the hierarchy. Let us explore this hypothesis with data from three countries:

the United States, Australia, and Sweden. The basic conclusion is that while there is strong evidence for a general gender gap in authority—the odds of women having authority are less than those of men—there is no evidence for systematic glass ceiling effects in the United States and only weak evidence for such effects in the other two countries. It describes the problem: the glass ceiling is a barrier so subtle that it is transparent, yet so strong that it prevents women from moving up the corporate hierarchy. From their vantage point on the corporate ladder, women can see the high-level corporate positions but are kept from reaching the top and *(Breaking the Glass Ceiling).*

The glass ceiling is not simply a barrier for an individual, based on the person's inability to handle a higher-level job. Rather, the glass ceiling *applies to women as a group* who are kept from advancing higher *because they are women.*

What causes the glass ceiling? Here is what women executives think.

Job Segregation Runs Rampant

Just as the overall labour market remains sharply segregated by sex, women executives are concentrated into certain types of jobs - mostly staff and support jobs - that offer little opportunity for getting to the top. A 1986 *Wall Street Journal* survey found The highest ranking women in most industries are in non-operating areas such as personnel, public relations, or, occasionally, finance specialties that seldom lead to the most powerful top-management posts. Women are locked out of jobs in the business mainstream, the route taken by CEOs and presidents. But even when women can get a line job, it is not likely to be in a crucial part of the business or the type of job that can mark them as leaders.

Dominance of the Old-Boy Network

According to one executive recruiter, the biggest barrier to women in top management levels is the bunch of guys sitting together around a table making all the decisions. In short, when deciding who to promote into management, male corporate leaders tend to select people as much like themselves as possible - so it is no surprise that women are frequently not even considered at promotion time. Instead, the men at the top look to former colleagues and old school ties; in both areas, women have been virtually absent.

Women executives are frequently excluded from social activities and often describe the clubbiness among the men that exists at the top. The corporate executive suites are the ultimate boys' clubs.

Even on a more formal level, women report there are certain kinds of meetings they don't get invited to because they are not seen as policy-makers. Corporate women don't travel on business as frequently as men, according to surveys by Korn/ Ferry Intemational (1982) and *Wall Street Joumal*/Gallup (1984). Studies confirm these differences in status and the different treatment of women. One study found that among executives at the same level, men managed greater numbers of people, had more freedom to hire and fire, and had more direct control of the company's assets than women.

Gender Discrimination

In the *Wall Street Journal*/Gallup survey, women managers were asked what they consider to be the most serious obstacle in their business careers. *Only 3 per cent cited family responsibilities,* but half named reasons related to their gender, including: male chauvinism, attitudes toward a female boss, slow advancement for women, and the *simple fact of being a woman.* In the survey by Korn/Ferry International, executive women were asked to name the greatest obstacle they had to overcome to achieve success; the most frequent response was simply being a woman (40 per cent). In a recent poll of 12,000 workers by the *Los Angeles Times*, two-thirds reported sex discrimination; 60 per cent saw signs of racism.

Most women aspiring to senior management positions believe the glass ceiling to career progression still exists, according to a report by a leading UK management organisation.

The survey of 3,000 members of the Institute of Leadership and Management (ILM) found 73 per cent of female respondents felt barriers still existed for women seeking senior management and board-level positions in the UK. In contrast, just 38 per cent of men believed there is a glass ceiling.

The report, Ambition and Gender at Work, suggests women's managerial career aspirations lag behind men's at every stage of their working lives, and that they have less clarity over traditional career direction than men.

At the start of their careers, 52 per cent of male managers had a fair or clear idea that they wanted to work in a particular role, compared with 45 per cent of women managers. Only half of women said they expected to become managers, versus two-thirds of men. Even among the under-30s, gender aspirations remained entrenched, with 45 per cent of men and 30 per cent of women expecting to become managers or leaders.

The findings, which came from an even sample of men and women with an average age of 43, also revealed that 24 per cent of women under 30 expected to start their own businesses within 10 years, compared with 20 per cent of men.

An institute's chief executive, said the pressure on many women to combine childcare with career aspirations was part of the cocktail. If large organisations wanted to nurture the talent of their best female employees, they needed to start challenging some of the unwritten rules of what senior management roles looked like.

It is not that women are risk-averse; younger women in particular are incredibly ambitious around entrepreneurial activity. Yet we can see that a promotion path within a large organisation is almost seen as riskier for them, on a personal basis, than going out and setting up their own venture, she said.

Companies have to think about how they can nurture that ambition. The only way is to hold chairmen and chief executives responsible. Good governance is good governance and it shouldn't be gender-specific.

A separate recent report by the London School of Economics for cosmetics company Avon predicted a doubling in young female entrepreneurs over the next decade, with 72 per cent of the 2,000 16-24-year-old women questioned saying the idea of being their own boss appealed to them.

If women can be there on booses i believe than believed young women would define the next generation of entrepreneurship and rewrite the rules in this perceived male-dominated world.

The trend towards more women entrepreneurs sent out a message about the need for change to the overall design of work. One of the reasons women want to set up businesses is because they have more control over the hours they work, she said.

There is plenty of evidence that in many UK workplaces there was discrimination, particularly against those who choose to be mothers, and also against those who choose non-traditional patterns of work.

Lord Davies's report into why Britain's boardrooms are so male-dominated, reportedly urge FTSE 100 companies to set voluntary targets for appointing female executives rather than imposing quotas, a policy that operates successfully in Norway and other countries.

Just under half of women responding to the Institute of Leadership and Management (UK) survey were in favour of boardroom quotas, although enthusiasm for the idea rose among the over 45s, with two-thirds of older women workers supporting the idea.

Imposing boardroom quotas is an admission of failure for business leaders. If early predictions about the Lord Davies review are correct, UK businesses have two years to increase the number of women on their boards, she said.

Rather than waiting for external legislation, now is the time for employers to set voluntary targets for female representation at board and senior management level, and hold people accountable for meeting them. Business leaders must take responsibility for building an effective talent pipeline, and make it a commercial priority to proactively identify, develop and promote potential leaders of both sexes.

The Fawcett Society is an organization in the United Kingdom that campaigns for women's rights and equality in Britain. The organisation's roots date back to 1866 when Millicent GarretFawcett campaigned for women's Suffrage, said: The report highlights just how far we have got to go on workplace equality between women and men. A lot of things come together to keep women out of leadership roles.

Outdated stereotypes about men and women's different roles in the workplace have an insidious effect on our cultural attitudes about who should do which jobs.

The lack of high profile women role models can make it hard for both women and men to imagine women running the show.

The world of work has not caught up with the needs of modern families where both parents work, with few senior positions offering flexibility around working hours – and it is still on the whole women who require flexibility in order to manage childcare commitments, thus restricting their career. Sexism, including women being passed over for top jobs, serves to further reinforce the glass ceiling.

All this can limit women's expectations for their career and acts as a brake on ambition.

She went on: Many years of tapping away at the glass ceiling have left it stubbornly intact. It is time we put aside our drip-drip tactics and took bold action to achieve real change.

Boardroom quotas are a radical – but not unthinkable means of bringing about a dramatic shift in the role of women in business.

They are not an end in themselves, and must be part of a package of measures designed to create a more representative and successful business norm – for example, there must also be wider awareness of incidental discrimination, and action to tackle it. But one only has to look at the success enjoyed by those countries that have embraced quotas to see it makes business sense.

So what does it take to ascend the slippery ladder- a very great deal. First of all women have to self motivate them-selves. What are the major issues in organising people. A woman manager is involved in managing workers, materials, processes and their interactions managing materials is a function of knowledge of the techniques such as planning financial budgeting programme Evaluation Revue Technic PERT and Critical Path Met CPM Program evaluation Review Technique and critical path methods for planning, organising, coordinating and executing the work.

What exactly is motivation? Women have natural people skills and soft skills which come into play in their constant interactions with superiors and subordinate staff in the office. With subordinate staff they have to help in ensuring that the understanding of the tasks they are required to fulfil is clear, what is the precise responsibility must be made clear at the stage of job design to ensure accountability. She has to allocate and supervise the work help in planning the work provide guidance and counselling and periodically appraise the quality of the work. As a professional she has to take orders from superiors to execute them through her team and constantly interact with peers and colleagues in the process. Thus, her management style will be coloured by these constant interactions. She has to understand behaviour of employees linked to their needs. The processes of job enrichment, motives needs to create an enabling environment where a climate of necessary self-actualisation is created where autonomy, individuation and collective action can move in tandem the staff are allowed to perform to their maximum capacity with full commitment to task employer organisation. It is important to have an understanding of what makes people tick. Working groups resemble individuals though they are always unique yet they share like individuals certain needs. All behaviour is goal directed. They aim to achieve certain things. These goals deal with physiological needs, psychological needs or higher order needs

First in the hierarchy of needs are the physiological needs of hunger, thirst, sleep, until these needs are satisfied to an optimal level they cannot move to the second order of needs these are needs of safety, security and protection from danger human beings need the security that their physiological needs will always be satisfied. They will continue to enjoy job security to fulfil their most basic needs. Once the second order needs

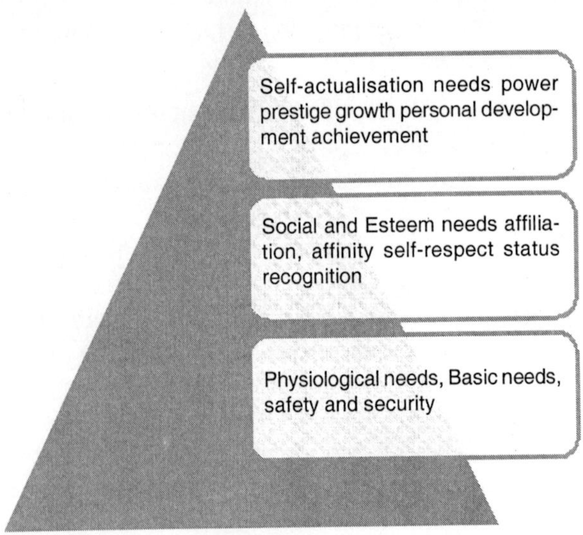

are fulfilled they graduate to the third order needs of affinity affiliation to an organisation in which they can subsume their personalities a larger calling the needs of love and belongingness once these needs are satisfied higher order needs of self-actualisation, recognition motivate people, women are by nature better placed to understand and instinctually respond to these needs and successfully harness these energies for the greater good of the greatest number and for the larger benefit of the organisation and the goals it seeks to sub-serve Hierarchy of human needs Abraham Maslow.

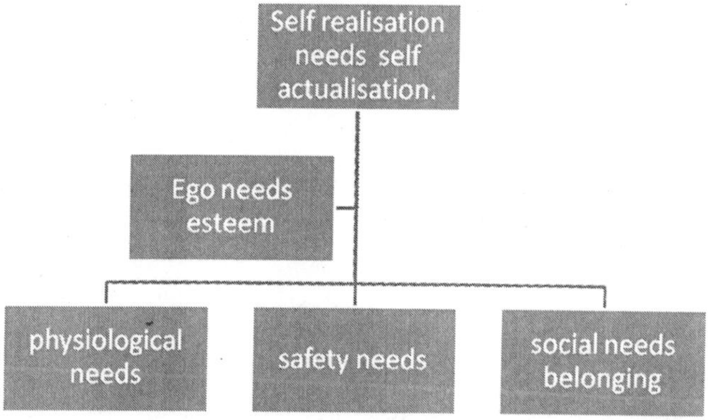

Maslow's hierarchy of needs is a theory in psychology proposed by Abraham Maslow in his paper written in 1943 a theory of human motivation Maslow uses the terms physiological safety, belongings love, esteem actualisation and self-transcendence to describe the pattern that human motivations generally more through. Maslow's theory was fully expressed in his book on Motivation and Personally written in 1954.

Maslow categorises the main needs of human beings into five: Women must equip themselves to be fully cognisant of the professional and technical aspects of the work of the Companies whose Boards they direct. Their leadership and man management skills need to be perfectly honed. Besides the commercial activities of the firm they must have a good knowledge of its administration and administrative details, promotion, placement and job rotation policies as these can influence morale and the overall productivity of the company. These also comprise the analytical requirements of the work they are required to take up additionally they need to increase contacts with people both within the company and outside up down and laterally their written and spoken communication must also posses necessary clarity.

Physiological or Bodily needs: The individual moves up the ladder responding first to the immediate satisfaction of his physiological needs. These are equated with pay rate and the physical conditions of the job. The next in the hierarchy are the safety needs, the need to be free from danger either from people or from the environment.

Safety: The individual needs the security of knowing that once his bodily needs are satisfied they will continue to be satisfied for the foreseeable future. He needs the security which provident fund and pension offer. The safety needs may take the form of job security, security against disease, old age, industrial injury such needs are generally met by safety laws, measure of social security protective labour laws and collective agreements.

Social Needs: Every employee needs to feel he is wanted and that he is not alone facing a hostile group. This is his need for being part of a group or of a team which helps him to identify with the larger organisation.

Ego or esteem needs: These needs are reflected in the desire for status and recognition, respect and prestige in the workgroup or work place such as is fulfilled through promotion and the workers need for positive strokes for a job well done. More important this means the generation within the employee of a feeling that at all times he enjoys the confidence of his superiors, the respect of his peers and colleagues. His contribution to the organisations goal is recognised he as an individual is recognised. Whether he becomes the secretary of the sports club, the President of the colony welfare association or the head of the Trade Union or an organisational body the same needs of recognition and affiliation are being fulfilled.

Self-actualisation: Needs the highest need is a function of self realisation and leadership. At this juncture of career the employee is able to jettison his dependence on others and on the larger corporate environment. He becomes the leader and not the follower he is able to impart thorough leadership and go forward. He becomes growth oriented, self-directed, detached and creative. This need reflects the extent to which an individual achieves the full flowering of her personality it has no exogenous influence it is purely endogenous. The individual herself needs to test her own limits. She needs to reach the full fruition of personality and to become a role model for others. She must learn to fly but like Icarus not too close to the sun.

Chapter 6

Leadership Styles of Men and Women

- Successful women describing their leadership styles often as: transformational – getting workers to transform or subordinate their individual self-interests into group consensus directed towards broader organisational goals.
- Others suggest female managers are more situation-based-adapting their strategies to the contingencies of the situation. Whereas men are more likely to view their leadership style as Transactional – jobs are seen as involving a series of transactions between themselves and their subordinates, leading to rewards or punishment.
- *Flattening structures and requiring more participative management, which style would best suit this environment?*
- Power attributed by personal characteristics: charisma, personal contacts and some suggest women with their natural style enabling them to lead and manage successfully within this new corporate environment compared to more male-dominated pyramid-shaped hierarchy.

- However, women in upper management positions are mainly in HR and communication/public relations where their "softer" participative style of management is viewed as better utilised.
- Interpersonal skills rather than organisation structure. To overcome barriers women need to communicating effectively, exceeding performance expectations, and building positive relationships with managers and colleagues and emphasise greatly on networking and mentoring, balancing home life and career.
- Over-come the sense of Isolation and loneliness
- Constant awareness of being a woman in man's world
- Lack of access to male networks
- Having to prove oneself to others
- Consistently exceed performance expectations
- Develop a style with which male managers feel comfortable
- Seek out challenging and visible assignments
- Obtain support from an influential mentor
- Having to work harder and be better than male counter-parts to need to work twice as hard to be considered half as good.
- Buttner (2001) reports that the management styles of women entrepreneurs was best described **using relational dimensions such as mutual empowering, collaboration, sharing of information, empathy and nurturing. Importantly, these dimensions, which have also been associated with women in different professional occupations**, were deemed to be associated with firm performance. Women do work differently from men. According to Heffernan (2003), **female negotiating styles have been shown to be different** and it has been demonstrated that they are significantly more beneficial to long-term business success. The most recent study that explored a genetic

basis for special attributes of women in social ability and empathy imply a better performance of companies created and run by women because of their ability to communicate better with employees, suppliers and customers. Women who exhibit superior competence on a task exert more influence than women who prove themselves less competent than superior women.

- Women are thought to be caring , tolerant, emotional, gentle and predisposed towards collaboration empowerment, teamwork whereas men are supposed to be aggressive, analytical, decisive and more inclined to act independently. These are really stereotypes think Scarlett O'Hara and Rhett Butler from Gone with the Wind, though Rhett Butler does say, We're one of a kind if I had to choose who was more hard as nails between them I would choose Scarlett. Having said that let me revert to this review of literature. In their study Transformational Transactional and Laisser Faire Leadership Styles Comparing Women and Men by Alice Heaglt and Mary C Johnson Schmitt of North Western University and Engen of Tillburge University said that As more woken enter Leadership Roles in society the possibility they might carry out these roles differently than men attracted increasing attention, women's behaviour is under scrutiny, in part, because they do not often rise to elite high level positions but continue to struggle and struggle in lower level positions. This is easily documented. As per the US Bureau of Labour Statistics the following is women's position. 46 per cent managers and administrators, fortune 500 companies 5 per cent of top corporate officers and 1 per cent of CEOs, A meta analysis of 45 studies of transformational, transactional, and Laissez Faire Leadership styles found that female leaders were more transformational than male-leaders and also engaged in more of the contingent behaviours that are a component of transactional leadership, male leaders were generally more inclined to exhibit passive management by exception and Laissez Faire Leadership. Although these differences between male and female leaders were small, the implications of these studies/ findings are encouraging for female leadership. Research has established that all the aspects of leadership style where women exceed men relate positively to leader's effectiveness whereas all of the aspects on which men exceeded women have negative or no relations to effectiveness. Eagly, Johnannsen-Scmidt and Von Engen in 2003 found that transformational leadership is practiced more often by women than by men. Transformational leadership is defined as establishing oneself as a role model to gain the confidence and trust of followers. Transformational leadership works better for females due to their demand for caring and supportive behaviours. Institutionalising women in leadership positions will make acceptance easier and remove the inherent advantage that men enjoy in their easier acceptability as natural leaders. Women are under pressure to perform well when they are part of a male group and also when they are tasked with leading such a group. Women have a greater concern for using power and lower self-esteem which inhibits them from reaching senior positions. People's expectations of their leader depending on the gender of the leader affects work environments differently. Women interestingly changed their leadership styles depending on whether they were leading a group of women or a group of men this innate resilience is also a vote for women's leadership. Women are the bridge between the team they lead and the manager they report to At one point only the macro picture or the helicopter view matters and at the other the nitty gritty of the ground level situation has to be understood and the worms eye view matters. Women are perhaps more successful leaders as they are able to keep their ears close to the ground and their eyes fixed on the big picture. This strategy pays off well but is generally restricted to middle management levels. They build strong teams line and staff function critical interrelation ship is clearly understood by them The strong team has the following components. There is a strong diverse seven to eight member team which meets regularly is passionate about its mission and generally has a champion which gives periodic updates and briefs the top management on the critical nature of the tasks being performed by the team to reach the goals as set out by the top management. Positive strokes caring sharing etc all work at mid management but where outcomes depend on independent strategic thinking and there are no collaborators only competitors women tend to falter. They have to build the necessary confidence in themselves to Dare to lead and not just ride the crest of a wave created by their followers. Though the capacity to earn the trust of their followers also marks them out. As women have high emotional quotients they find it easier to understand quirks and behavioural traits and find it easy to meld a team together The basic issue is that there is no one leadership style which is fixed this has to be mutable and largely contingent on the demands of the situation at hand.

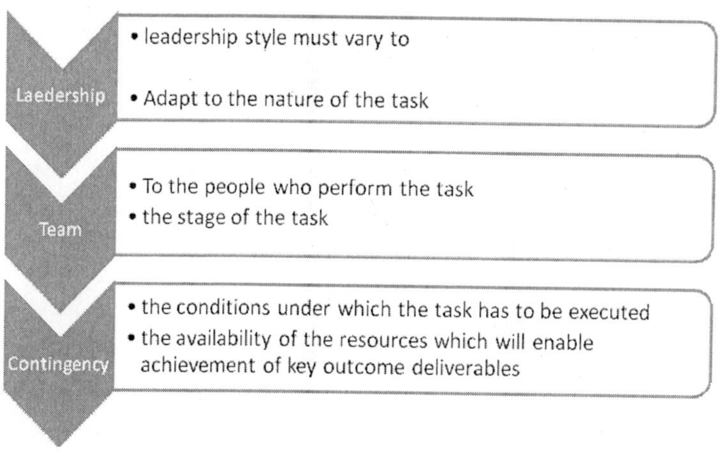

Thus, there are divergent forms of flexibility emotional verbal mental physical which are necessitated

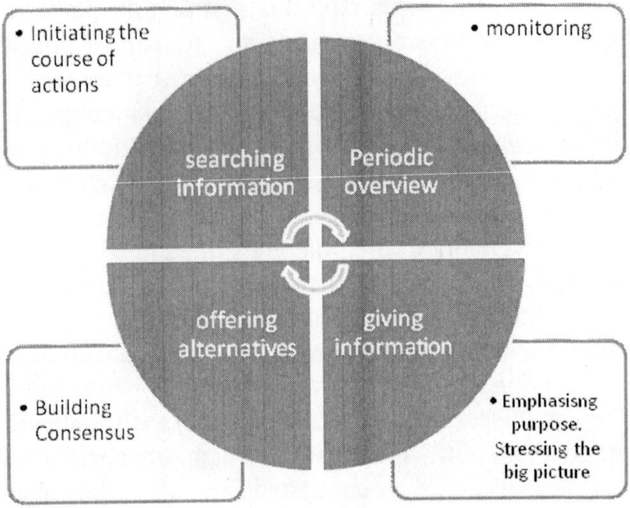

It is a long and carefully calibrated process as is often Repeated Coming together is a beginning keeping together is progress and working together and attaining the envisaged outcomes is success. Women are much better at maintenance of relationships.

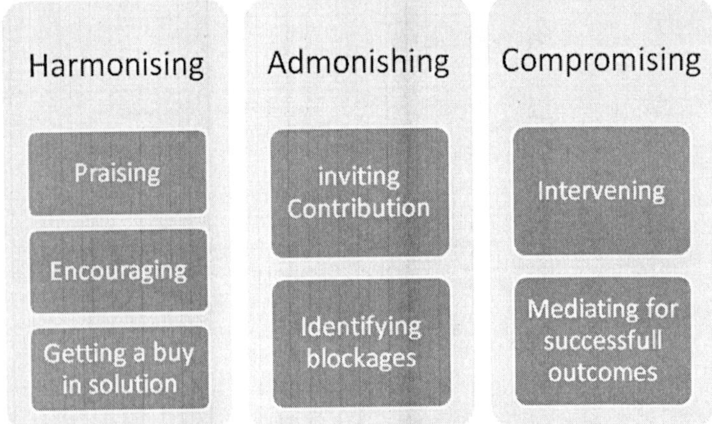

Thus, a degree of emotional competency along with professional calibre and job knowledge is essential to overcome the barriers which will always arise initially when a task is visualised and initiated. Women are better at working with people this has, in fact, been empirically established through a series of significant studies. The popular definition of a team becomes together each achieves more. Aligning tasks with talent is the key to success but difficult to do it necessitates serious listening allowing the articulation of dissent but within controlled parameters thus in the second table the admonishment to the team members is followed by an invitation to contribute their ideas are listened to with the respect and attention that they deserve and then they are encouraged to articulate divergent views which are used to identify and remove blockages. Compromise is initiated, there is a willingness to concede and an openness and lack of hostility in the process. It should not be viewed either as an attempt to score adversarial ad hominem brownie points or an attempt to paper over the cracks. It is essential to be able to understand the viewpoints of other team members and to keep an open mind. Sometimes for conflict resolution to be effective the leaders active intervention is necessitated this mediation results in goal attainment. The orchestration of all these phases in the cycle comes easily to women. There is also a lot to be said for synergy and subsuming the individual ego in the task at hand and allowing for maximum autonomy for fulfilment and satisfaction all this is well and good in peace time but at war in an extreme contingency everyone looks out for the masterful and dominating leader who will get them out of the mess they should not have gotten into in the first place. This is the inflection point women do not find themselves able to handle and which they should consciously prepare themselves to deal with Emotional Intelligence they are good with. This is a term coined by Daniel Goleman ultimately this is how emotional intelligence pans out technical skills 5 per cent Domain expertise 10 per cent attitude 85 per cent.

Management is a skill which can be taught as can leadership Women have to learn to mange themselves at the workplace first they must proceed with their work with a cool firm head on their shoulders with their feet wide and firmly planted on the ground it is essential to manage one's own emotions to emerge as a credible and emotionally mature leader take stress in their stride be full of energy, through the day and to be able to manage their time well.

As far as managing emotions is concerned you have to manage at several levels and planes of consciousness the biggest pitfall to be guarded against is anger it is just one step away from danger the Bhagavad-Gita explains it well

krodhad bhavati sammohah
sammohat smrti-vibhramah
smrti-bhramsad buddhi-naso
buddhi-nasat pranasyati

From anger, delusion arises, and from delusion bewilderment and confusion of memory. When memory is

bewildered confused intellect is confounded, intelligence is lost, and when intelligence is lost, one is lost. Therefore the good manager must keep anger at bay. Women must consciously work harder to master their emotions the emotions should not govern you. You should be able to master these seemingly uncontrollable passions.

To be charismatic is to have a vision and to have the ability to share that overarching vision with the line and staff. There are several such examples, John F Kennedy is one whom most people will find it easy to relate to Above all, he gave the world for an imperishable moment the vision of a leader who greatly understood the terror and the hope, the diversity and the possibility of life on this planet and who made people look beyond nation and race to the future of humanity. Today's leader will be under constant threat will be challenged by herself, by her employees, by customers by the print electronic and social media, by fast paced technological developments and so on. The rapidity of response will be dictated by the painstaking preparation for that response. Just as organisations think of themselves as living organisms which undergo processes of entropy and repair regard themselves as highly flexible responsive and responsible organisations as integrated and evolving systems so must those who helm these organisations be able to offer a clear vision and be able to respond easily and lucidly with erudition and also be able to evolve continuously both as leaders and as knowledge workers as lifelong learners. Thus, for women there are several mental barriers which they must learn to overcome to learn to trust but not too much to learn to jump but not too far to know and to use affiliation but not overmuch they must confront whatever impedes them head on and most of all it is the Goldilocks dilemma they must learn to get it exactly right for the win win outcomes through strong teams and an unshakable belief in the overarching idealistic macro vision in honesty, fairness and idealism and sure they will get there.

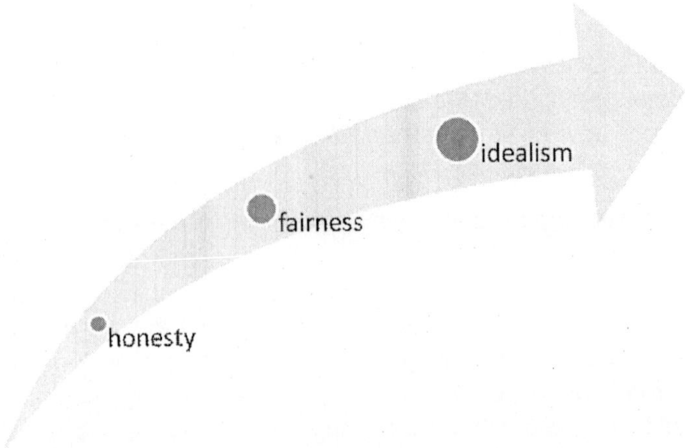

A lot also depends on the personality of the person handling the situation hence an understanding of personality of women also becomes important.

THEORIES OF PERSONALITY

Carl Jung identified three basic assumptions in his theory. (1) Personalities are developmental in that they are influenced by past and hopes for the future. (2) All people have the potential for growth and change. (3) Personality is the totality of a person's interacting sub-systems.

Emotional Orientations

Jung feels that the two basic Orientations of People are extroversion and introversion. Introverts are primarily oriented to the subjective world. They look inward at themselves, avoid social contacts and initiating interaction with others, withdrawn, quiet and enjoy solitude. Extroverts are friendly, enjoy interaction with people, are generally aggressive and express feelings and ideas openly.

Fig. 1.1: Extroverts versus Introverts: Characteristics of Each

Extroverts	***Introverts***
Like variety and action	Like quiet for concentration.
Tend to work faster, dislike complicated procedure.	Tend to be careful with details, dislike sweeping statements.
Are often good at greeting people.	Have trouble remembering names and faces.
Are often impatient with long slow jobs.	Tend not to mind working on one project for a long time uninterruptedly.
Are interested in results of their job, getting it done and in how other people do it.	Are interested in the idea behind their in job.
Often do not mind interruption of answering the telephone.	Dislike telephone intrusions and interruptions.
Often act quickly, sometimes without thinking.	Like to think a lot before they act, sometimes without acting.
Like to have people around.	Work contentedly alone.
Usually communicate freely.	Have some problems communicating.

Managers should gain an understanding of themselves and learn how understanding other scan make them better managers.

Validity results showed that introvert/extrovert is really applicable to only the rare extremes. Most individuals tend to be ambiverts, that is, they are in between introversion and extroversion.

Problem-solving Styles

Jung identified two basic steps in problem-solving: collecting information and making a decision. Collecting data occurs in a continuum from sensing to intuition. In terms of decision-making, it ranges from 'thinking' to 'feeling' types.

Sensing type: The person approaches the problem in a step by step organised way. The person works steadily and patiently with details.

Intuitive type: One who does not show a lot of emotion, who can put things in a logical order and who can be firm and fair.

The feeling type is very aware of other people, dislikes telling people unpleasant things and prefers harmony among people.

The interaction of these two aspects of problem-solving results in four problem-solving types.

(1) The sensing-feeling person likes to collect data in an orderly way and make decisions that take into account the needs of people. This person is very concerned with high-quality decisions that people will accept and implement.

(2) The intuitive-feeling person is equally concerned with the people side of decisions but the focus is on new ideas which are often broad in scope and lacking in details.

(3) Sensing-thinkers emphasise details and the quality of a decision. They are not as concerned with the people aspect of an organisation as with a technically sound decision.

(4) Intuitive-thinking types like to tackle new and innovative problems, but make decisions primarily on technical terms. They tend to be good planners, but not so good at implementing.

(5) There is always a combination of these types in a person.

General attitudes: The last personality sub-system Jung identified was the general attitude toward work, namely judging and perceptive. Judging types like to follow a plan, like to make decisions, and want only the essentials for their work. On the other hand, perceptive types adapt well to change, want to know all about a job and may get overcommitted.

Fig. 1.2: Sensing Types versus Intuitive Types: Characteristics of Each

Sensing Types MARS(MEN)	*Intuitive Types VENUS (WOMEN)*
Dislike new problems unless there are standard ways to solve them.	Like solving new problems.
Like an established way of doing things.	Dislike doing the same thing repeatedly.
Enjoy using skills already learned more than learning new ones.	Enjoy learning a new skill more than using it.
Work more steadily, with realistic idea of how long it will take.	Work in bursts of energy powered by enthusiasm, with slack periods in between.
Usually reach a conclusion step by step.	Reach a conclusion quickly.
Are patient with routine details.	Are impatient with routine details.
Are impatient when the details get complicated.	Are patient with complicated situations.
Are not often inspired, and rarely trust the inspiration when they are.	Follow their inspirations, good or bad.
Seldom make errors of fact.	Frequently make errors of fact.
Tend to be good at precise work.	Dislike taking time for decision.

Fig. 1.3: Thinking Types versus Feeling Types: Characteristics of Each

Thinking Types	*Feeling Types*
Do not show emotion readily and are often uncomfortable dealing with people's feelings.	Tend to be very aware of other people and their feelings.
May hurt people's feelings without knowing it.	Enjoy pleasing people, even in unimportant things.
Like analysis and putting things into logical order; can get along without harmony.	Like harmony, Efficiently may be badly disturbed by office feuds.
Tend to decide impersonally, sometimes paying insufficient attention to people's wishes.	Often let decisions be influenced by their own or other people's personal likes and wishes.
Need to be treated fairly.	Need occasional praise.
Are able to reprimand people or fire them when necessary.	Dislike telling people unpleasant things.

(Contd...)

Are more analytically oriented; respond more easily to people's thoughts.	Are more people-oriented; respond more easily to people's values.
Tend to be firm-minded	Tend to be sympathetic.

Fig. 1.4: Judging Types versus Perceptive Types: Characteristics of Each

Judging Types	*Perceptive Types*
Work best when they can plan their work and follow the plan.	Adapt well to changing situations
Like to get things settled and finished.	Do not mind leaving things open for alterations.
May decide things too quickly.	May have trouble making decisions.
May dislike to interrupt the project they are on for a more urgent one.	May start too many projects and have difficulty finishing them.
May not notice new things that need to be done.	May postpone unpleasant jobs.
Want only the essentials needed to begin their work.	Want to know all about a new job.
Tend to be satisfied once they reach ajudgement on a thing, situations or person.	Tend to be curious and welcome new information on a thing, situation or person.

Chapter 7

Learning to Handle Power

Power is not a dirty word it can be leveraged to benefit others or to corrupt processes to self-serving short end self-goals. Women have to learn to be comfortable with the judicious exercise of power if they see themselves as the numero uno Imperious Maximus. There is a currency of power which comes from interlocking obligations. Every time you do something to help another person you generate some currency like the Godfather you can use it at any point in the immediate present or the distant future or never use it. Just know that you have it if required. If you go out of your way for someone he will also go the extra mile for you this is the inbuilt reciprocity which obligations engender. Women are not good at using this currency and are almost embarrassed to acknowledge that they even own it and yet it is essential to have to, use to, perpetuate power and build relationships of trust based on its judicious exercise. Respected you will be secure, honoured and successful. A leader who thinks more about his own interest than about yours, who seeks his own advantage for everything he does will never be a good leader for others will never be able to trust him. The leader must be able to exercise reward power point out the what's in it for me WIIFM factor wanting to know how you will benefit from a given proposal is natural it does not mean you are selfish or unethical or unconcerned about others, quite simply you cannot afford the luxury of being any of these things, It is a natural response to a new idea and you need to know what is in it for me. The word power is then defined as something we use to affect positive change it can be used for the largest common good. As leaders we have to understand power its use its abuse its limits and we must be governed by ethical standards in the exercise of this power. You frequently hear the expression stakeholders and contextually it is said to be a Win Win Situation. So if it's a win win situation are there just two people who win or can the larger

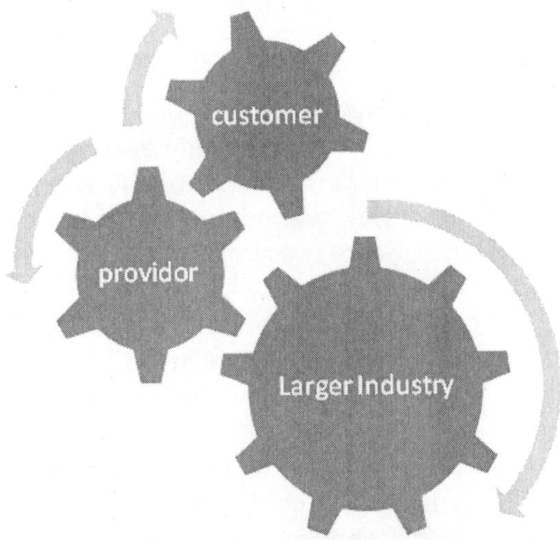

organisation also benefit. There is a very simple touchstone is the behaviour ethical are you persuading your team to do or not do something in a principled way. If you or your followers are persuaded to act in an unethical way the entire process becomes suspect and the mission is aborted as tainted. Once uncovered it will irredeemably tarnish your own reputation and that of your Company or the organisation that you work for so in the long term the end quite simply does not justify the means and is not worth it. There are a few quick questions against which actions can reasonably be judged.

By doing this what ethical by

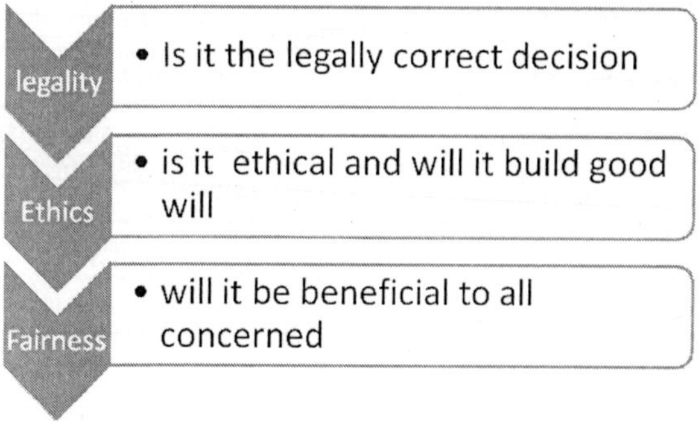

By initiating this action what ethical message am I sending or failing to send to others?

Do people know what to do or whom to turn to when they have ethical concerns. Is this a grey area is it completely legal is it ethical if yes would I be comfortable taking this decision if my family were watching. If it were to be a newspaper headline tomorrow. Who is the primary beneficiary who is the secondary beneficiary of this action.

Types of thinking: The most easily understood terms for divergent and convergent thinking Men are from Mars women are from Venus are left brain and right brain thinking. Whatever you term it the difference as also the plausible need for both types of thinking needs to be accepted. Divergent problem-solving is intuitive creative and spontaneous. Divergent thinkers see what everyone else is not seeing. They are most often subjective as opposed to being cool dispassionate and objective Their thinking is different and out of the box they juxtapose different elements and take on different roles by personifying problems.

Right Brain and Left Brain Characteristics

Left Hemisphere Style	*Right Hemisphere Style*
Rational • Responds to verbal instructions	**Intuitive** • Responds to demonstrated instructions
• Problem solves by logically and sequentially looking at the parts of things	• Problem solves with hunches, looking for patterns and configurations
• Looks at differences	• Looks at similarities
• Is planned and structured	• Is fluid and spontaneous
• Prefers established, certain information	• Prefers elusive, uncertain information
• Prefers talking and writing	• Prefers drawing and manipulating objects
• Prefers multiple choice tests	• Prefers open ended questions
• Controls feelings	• Free with feelings
• Prefers ranked authority structures	• Prefers collegial authority structures
Sequential • Is a splitter: distinction important	**Simultaneous** • Is a lumper: connectedness important
• Is logical, sees cause and effect	• Is analogic, sees correspondences, resemblances
Draws on previously accumulated, organised information	Draws on unbounded qualitative patterns that are not organised into sequences, but that cluster around images

These are popular stereotypes of how men think logically and dispassionately with the left brain and women think passionately and creatively with the right brain. This may or may not be true but what is however undeniable is that the organisation needs both skills and competencies and women must therefore train themselves to think with the head more. Eventually what is needed is just a safe pair of hands. Mars and Venus complement each other.

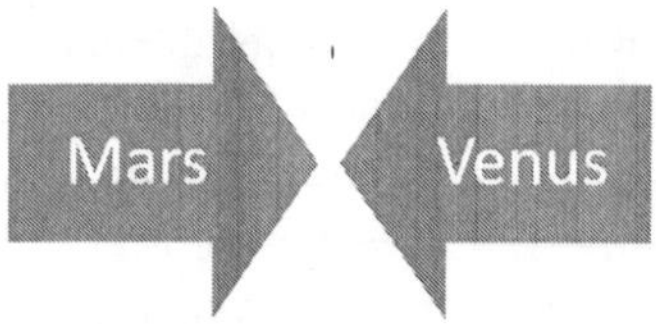

- *Managing Meetings* Every team needs people who are knowledgeable yet there are some who wear knowledge with an attitude chip on their shoulders women are generally better at managing such people and getting the best out of them.

Managing Meetings

Managing Meetings. Managing Meeting is a way of conflict resolution, allowing for different opinions to emerge but not for open conflicts.

The best way to do this is to limit the time the person expounds; he does not have a divine right to dominate the meeting. He will otherwise do just this as a right and edge out all those who may have equally good ideas. The omniscient owl can also be asked to make written submissions that can be discussed in a question answer session to test their practicability in a meeting. He can be used to mentor the younger officers who can benefit from his expertise. They also easily identify lambs. Those poor folk who have good ideas but would rather blend into the wood work than choose to speak up. Women leaders often choose to bring such people out firstly by praising whatever sensible remark they are persuaded to make and then speaking to the introverted person privately explaining that their contribution to the team is value addition then there are Hyenas who would like to disrupt all serious business lacing it with levity. A time monitor for the meeting can keep the discussion serious and time focussed and keeps the hyena in place. There are also Lions who will try to bully their way through. For women leaders it is important to always stand up to their King of the jungle complex generally though occasionally give them charge of a single project and closely monitor execution of the same so their roar is matched with measurable, monitorable, deliverable outcomes on the ground. There are queen bees who want to hide in the hive and slough off all real work onto someone else. These must also be firmly dealt with thus by cleverly managing these five animals who are present in all meetings, the omniscient owl, the lamb, the hyena, the lion, and the queen bee women leaders can be successful. An active confident positive leader there will be an innate sense of fulfilment in being able to bloom and exercise all your skills.

- Women make up 50 per cent of the workforce have higher educational attainments than men in the emerging market economies they are the primary bread-winners in their families, despite this they are underrepresented at the workplace in senior managerial positions and definitely in top leadership positions. The Organisation for economic Cooperation and Development asserts that if developed countries raised the employment level of women to that of men they could increase their GDP by 12 per cent by 2030 other studies as the recent survey by Mc Kinsey and Co show that having more women at the workplace increases productivity and efficiency. Women do not need help they need recognition and support. They need champions. They have similar qualifications, capabilities and education as men. Companies need to have a strategic framework for gender diversity with goals, targets, sponsors and support networks and with clear leadership from the top. Engagement with Women employees' enablement and encouragement these are the three Es which she recommends for creating a talent pipeline enhancing capabilities and bringing women to the forefront.

We've all heard the claims, the theories, and the speculation about the ways leadership styles vary between women and men.

The Harvard Business Review (May, 2012) data come from 360 evaluations, so what they are tracking is the judgment of a leader's peers, bosses, and direct reports. They asked these individuals to rate each leader's effectiveness overall and also to judge how strong he or she is on the 16 competencies that 30 years of research show are most important to overall leadership effectiveness. Ask, for instance, how good a leader is at taking the initiative, developing others, inspiring and motivating, and pursuing their own development.

The latest survey of 7,280 leaders, which the organisation evaluated in 2011, confirms some seemingly eternal truths about men and women leaders in the workplace but also holds some surprises. The dataset was generated from leaders in some of the most successful and progressive organisations in the world both public and private, government and commercial, domestic and international.

In the confirmation category is its first finding: The majority of leaders (64 per cent) are still men. And the higher the level, the more men there are: In this group, 78 per cent of top managers were men, 67 per cent at the next level down (that is, senior executives reporting directly to the top managers), 60 per cent at the manager level below that.

Similarly, most stereotypes would have us believe that female leaders excel at "nurturing" competencies such as developing others and building relationships and many might put exhibiting integrity and engaging in self-development in that category as well. And in all four cases the data concurred — women did score higher than men.

But the women's advantages were not at all confined to traditionally women's strengths. In fact, at every level, more women were rated by their peers, their bosses, their direct reports, and their other associates as better overall leaders than their male counterparts — and the higher the level, the wider that gap grows:

Overall Leadership Effectiveness by Gender by Position (Percentile Scores)

	Male	*Female*
Tom Management, Executive, Senior Team Members	57.7	67.7
Reports to Top Management, Supervises Middle Managers	48.9	56.2
Middle Manager	49.9	52.7
Supervisor, Front Line Manager, Foreman	52.5	52.6
Individual contributor	52.7	53.9
Other	50.7	52.0
Total	**51.3**	**55.1**

Source: Zenger Folkman Inc., 2011.

Specifically, at all levels, women are rated higher in fully 12 of the 16 competencies that go into outstanding leadership. Two of the traits where women outscored men to the highest degree — taking initiative and driving for results — have long been thought of as particularly male strengths. As it happened, men outscored women significantly on only one management competence in this survey — the ability to develop a strategic perspective.

So what should we conclude from these data? Why are we not engaging and fully employing these exemplary women leaders? Yes, blatant discrimination is a potential explanation, if not actual than certainly perceptual. When the survey findings were with a group of women outside this particular survey and asked them to suggest why they thought their colleagues had been rated so highly on taking initiative and self-development,

The Top 16 Competencies Top Leaders Exemplify Most

	Male Mean Percentile	*Female Mean Percentile*	*T value*
Take Initiative	48	56	-11.58
Practices Self-Development	48	55	-9.45
Displays High Integrity and Honesty	48	55	-9.28
Drives for Results	48	54	-8.84
Develops Others	48	54	-7.94
Inspires and Motivates Others	49	54	-7.53
Builds Relationships	49	54	-7.15
Collaboration and Teamwork	49	53	-6.14
Establishes Stretch Goals	49	53	-5.41
Champions Change	49	53	-4.48
Solves Problems and Analyses Issues	50	52	-2.53
Communicates Powerfully and Prolifically	50	52	-2.47
Connects the Group to the Outsides World	50	51	-0.78
Innovates	50	51	-0.76
Technical or Professional Expertise	50	51	-0.11
Develops Strategic Perspective	51	49	2.79

Source: Zenger Fokman Inc., 2011.

their answers pointed to the still-tenuous position they feel themselves to be in the workplace:

We need to work harder than men to prove ourselves.

We feel the constant pressure to never make a mistake, and to continually prove our value to the organisation.

That is, anecdotally, at least, the women queried don't feel their appointments are safe. They're afraid to rest on their laurels. Feeling the need (often keenly) to take initiative, they are more highly motivated to take feedback to heart.

The irony is that these are fundamental behaviours that drive the success of *every* leader, whether woman or man.

Why are women viewed as less strategic? This is an easier question to answer. Top leaders always score significantly higher in this competency; since more top leaders are men, men still score higher here in the aggregate. But when measured only men and women in top management on strategic perspective, their relative scores are the same.

What should leaders and managers do with these findings? Here are some thoughts.

- As leaders in organisations look hard to find the talent they need to achieve exceptional results, they ought to be aware that many women have impressive leadership skills. Research shows these leadership skills are strongly correlated to organisational success factors such as retaining talent, customer satisfaction, employee engagement, and profitability.
- As to the constant state of unease we hear women leaders express — clearly, chauvinism or discrimination is an enigma that organisations (and the business culture) should work hard to prevent. However, that said, think of the benefits every leader in every organisation would gain from a mind-set that they simply can't afford to make a mistake. Paranoia or extreme risk aversion is clearly detrimental to a rising career. But in today's economic climate, every leader, male or female, would do well to avoid becoming complacent.

  As a young psychology student I was fascinated by a picture which could be seen as that of an old woman or that of a young woman it introduced me to the idea of Gestalt seeing wholeness of things and so both things are there. There is a glass ceiling. With capability and innate confidence in one's own abilities without being naive one can smash it and get ahead but the colours black and white are both present in women's situation discrimination is there, it will always be there it is something that can be felt but cannot really be established. The idea of this book is not to deny it but to embrace it and in so doing unshackle the spirit and overcome it. Transcendence is illusory but overcoming the barriers to growth as a basis is real enduring and sustainable. Women leaders are more assertive and persuasive, have a stronger need to get things done and are more willing to take risks than male leaders.

Women leaders also were found to be more empathetic and flexible, as well as stronger in interpersonal skills than their male counterparts. ***These qualities combine to create a leadership style that is inclusive, open, consensus building, collaborative and collegial.***

- We should emphasise that the male leaders in this study were also exceptional in these areas. But the women leaders set a new standard..
- As a footnote, the women leaders in the United Kingdom and the United States share very similar, very strong profiles.

While scores of executives and academicians have weighed in on what it takes to be an effective leader, a participant in the study, provides an excellent working definition: ***Strong leadership starts with being able to pull together a group of people—who may not have anything in common—and getting them to buy into a vision of themselves as a collective group who can achieve uncommon results.*** Womanomics:

> Women are equal. Women can no longer be treated as disenfranchised excluded forgotten if economic efficiency and equity objectives are to be pursued seriously. This has happened large numbers of women have entered paid employment fought for and won civil rights. We have come a fairly long way but with immeasurable distance still to go.

Women Hold up half the sky Mao Tse Tung:

> Half the world's population comprises of women. Gender discrimination is a global phenomenon. Women

do not have access to land in most parts of the world and especially in South Asia China the Pacific, thus they are not able to put up the necessary collateral to avail of loans from mainstream financial institutions They lack access to Bank accounts and consequently to credit from mainstream financial institutions. Though they are producers and consumers of goods and services they remain poor and marginalised. Women with little that they can call their own poor and discriminated against with limited access to literacy, basic literacy and financial literacy sanitation and health. Essentially women lack opportunities which will allow and enable the full flowering of personality and enable them to realise their dreams. Several steps have been taken by the Indian Government to enable equal socio-economic participation of women a lot more needs to be done for achieving global standards of gender equality. Laws, policies, programmes and services are needed to achieve and implement these standards. While women's concerns is indeed a very large and challenging subject this book focuses on the need to make women economic actors able to transact in the public space by enhancing women's economic em-powerment. We need greater gender responsiveness and sensitivity in the formulation and implementation of macro policies for women. Gender responsiveness will become embedded only when larger numbers of women secure jobs in the market economy. While there is still a lot of focus on rural women urban women are still largely ignored as per the census figures of 2011 of the total population of 121.1 million about 377.1 million live in urban areas 195.8 are men and 181.2 women. In one decade 2001 and 2011 census figures ibid the ratio has increased from 900 women per 1000 men in 2001 to 925 women per 1000 men in 2011. Half the population in the cities comprises of women. We need cities where women also enjoy access to public spaces inclusive cities are those where women can work and transact in public spaces and enjoy freedom of movement free from molestation it is only when these basic freedoms are secured will women are able to access social, political and economic resources on equal footing with their male counterparts and power economic growth and development. The change in women's condition is significant though of course a lot needs to be done the initial occupation for women of Doctor, Nurse, Teacher, counter clerk, secretary have changed women are increasingly emerging as hardnosed corporate head honchos but the agenda is still incomplete and a lot still needs to be done.

Handling Power well is important

Handling immense power goes with the immense responsibilities women are required to handle at work

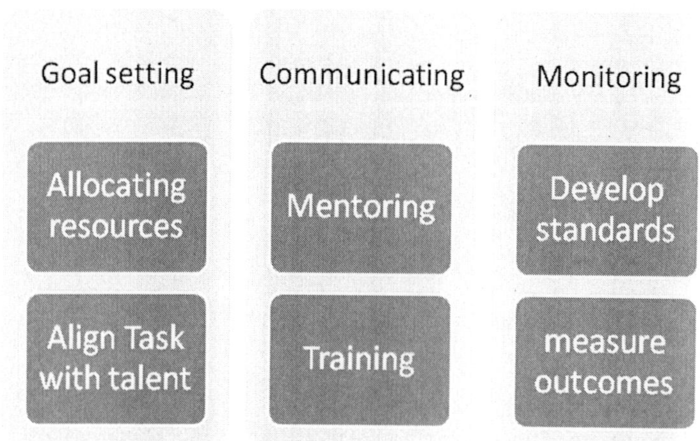

As a leader you have reward power and punishment power, you have to set the agenda, locate the people headhunt those who will operationalise it. Set the broader goals, allocate the resources. These can take the form of physical, material, money, human, resources. It is essential to align talent with task. Then instruct and train personnel build their professional competency, domain knowledge and capability to courageously execute the tasks within the defined timelines and finally develop standards against which the quality of outcomes are measurable. A different type of ABCD analysis is required to be initiated. At the very outset, In introducing the new project idea first (A) anticipate the objections then (B) benefitise people divide up the loaves and fishes. (C) Categorise think of all the individuals, (D) departments, groups, schedules, budgets, publicity locations etc that you need to consider and take care of D. Of course is to develop your plans to the last detail. Take pride in the individual and team achievements and create an Enabling atmosphere which allows all others to do the same. The key to leadership as is influence not authority.

Power struggles are the ugly face of business, you must constantly equip yourself to deal with them. The more power you have, the more people who are tied to you by obligation. This chain has to be forged upward and downward and laterally

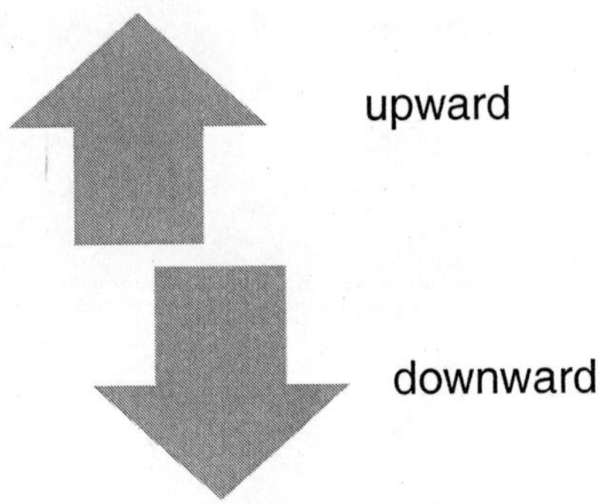

too the greater the power you will enjoy in the organisation, You have the loyalty of subordinates and the good grace of your superiors this is building up an arsenal to protect yourself in the inevitable power struggle which is bound to arise. You just have to build up your power base in part increasing others obligation to you.You can also reinforce that power by learning about the different types of power and increasing your clout in each dimension.

Power is my mistress. I have worked too hard at her conquest to allow anyone to take her away from me. Napoleon Bonaparte, 1804

Research over the past two decades has established the panoptic effect of power on people. Put simply: Power changes people. People who rise to the tops of companies and other organisations tend to prioritise their own goals and desires above those of others, fail to take other people's perspectives into account, tend to disregard other people's feelings and are, well, less polite. What most companies haven't recognised fully is the amount of damage these high-powered Napoleons can do, especially when the Napoleons must work together within the same team.

Research published over the past three years paints a bleak picture for organisations that ignore the damage that power run amok can do. When high-powered people work with teammates who are a potential threat, the high-powered people lash out. Conflict ensues. Because power is so valued, people within reach of the top tier of an organisation will fight to retain their position at the top. We find the power conflicts in management teams are so common that teams you'd expect to be the best, such as management teams, can actually be less effective than those lower down on the organisational chart.

At best, this is an enormous loss of potential for an organisation relying on its most skilled and experienced employees. At worst, conflicts result in firings and outright failures. Companies that ignore the power struggles eventually pay the price.

Research, published in *Organisational Behaviour and Human Decision Processes* and the *Journal of Applied Psychology*, suggests that companies look toward egalitarian models of management and leadership — think King Arthur, not Napoleon — to avoid or minimise power struggles within their top teams. Clarity is also important: Teams in which power and leadership roles are established clearly, and teams in which people's perceptions of their own power match their teammates' perceptions of it, perform better.

There are key differences in the way low-powered and high-powered teams function. In low-powered teams, hierarchy helps: Without a hierarchy, a power vacuum develops and the teams aren't sure which way to go. In management teams, a hierarchy, such as vice-presidents working with C-suite executives, or C-suite executives vying for the CEO slot, has the opposite effect. It gives ambitious women a ladder to fight over, increases the conflict and reduces effectiveness. Establishing an egalitarian culture in high-powered teams isn't easy. Organisations can change the environment in which the executives are operating, but they probably can't transform the characters of the executives or the addictive nature of power.

Research suggests three steps that organisations could take. King Arthur, when faced with a council of ambitious knights, brought peace to his team by building a round table. In the medieval legend, each knight had a role to play: Sir Lancelot was the greatest champion, Sir Galahad was the purest of heart, Sir Gareth killed the Red Knight and so on. Organisations can reduce conflict within their management teams by following a path toward shared power and clear roles.

1. **Define, discuss and reinforce roles.** Problems in management teams go away if team members can reach clear, accepted agreement over roles and standing and continue to reinforce those as time goes by. If a departing CEO names a successor, fighting among the lower executive ranks who are eyeing the top spot might be reduced. Conflict can also be better managed

when each team member's expertise is recognised and deferred to. A person who feels confident in his or her role is less likely to feel threatened.

2. **Establish shared decision-making.** Members of high-powered teams feel less threatened by other team members when decision-making is shared. Shared power reduces the real or perceived power differentials among members. Democratic decision-making styles, such as agreeing by consensus, or informal votes, are an aid here. The concept of servant leadership may serve a CEO well to help delegate decision-making.

Provide conflict training and create a culture of respect. Management teams that have sufficient training in conflict management skills are better at recognising conflict and addressing the real underlying issues. Power struggles often arise in discussion of tasks or seemingly mundane process matters, such as what day of the week meetings will be held. Teams can establish a culture of respect in those discussions; or find creative ways to expand the hierarchy pie, so that each person in the team has power, though perhaps not in the domain he or she wants. Recognising which team members are engaged in a power struggle and resolving it quickly and respectfully is artistry possessed by a few great leaders. Generally Empathetic woman are better at conflict resolution research shows how worthwhile it is for an organisation to invest in fostering that ability. Sometimes this struggle is departmental: Sales wants something from Marketing but Marketing isn't giving it to them so Sales yells louder, maybe with a threat or two for effect. Other times, the power battle is more personal: one team member wants something from another team member and tries to use her power to get it. Sometimes, even, it works.

But more often than not, it fails. Grabbing power, especially when you don't have it, is unpredictable, feels bad to both parties, and is bullying. The collateral damage to the relationship is almost always high. There's got to be a better way to get what you want when you're powerless in a situation.

Business leaders and board members who ignore power struggles within their management teams do so at the organisation's risk. Napoleon unchecked ravaged Europe. What are the deleterious effects unchecked Napoleons can have on the company? preserve their power, sometimes aggressively, when they feel that it is threatened.

Formal Power

Coercive

Coercive power is conveyed through fear of losing one's job, being demoted, receiving a poor performance review, having prime projects taken away, etc. This power is secured through threatening others. For example, the Vice President of Sales who threatens sales folks to meet their goals or get replaced.

Reward

Reward power is conveyed through rewarding individuals for compliance with one's wishes. This may be done through giving bonuses, raises, a promotion, extra time off from work, etc. For example, the supervisor who provides employees comp ensatory 'off' time when they meet an objective she sets for a project.

Legitimate

Legitimate power comes from having a position of power in an organisation, such as being the boss or a key member of a leadership team. This power comes when employees in the organisation recognise the authority of the individual.. For example, the CEO who determines the overall direction of the company and the resource needs of the company.

Personal Power

Expert

Expert power comes from one's experiences, skills or knowledge. As we gain experience in particular areas, and become thought leaders in those areas, we begin to gather expert power that can be utilised to get others to help us meet our goals. For example, the Project Manager who is an expert at solving particularly challenging problems to ensure a project stays on track.

Referent

Referent power comes from being trusted and respected. We can gain referent power when others trust what we do and respect us for how we handle situations. For example, the Human Resource Associate who is known for ensuring employees are treated fairly and coming to the rescue of those who are not.

Power tends to get to people's heads, psychologist Nicole Lipkin tells Business Insider. We're not really trained to handle power well.

Analysis uses the five types of power introduced by psychologists John French and Bertram Raven in 1959, along with two types that were introduced later.

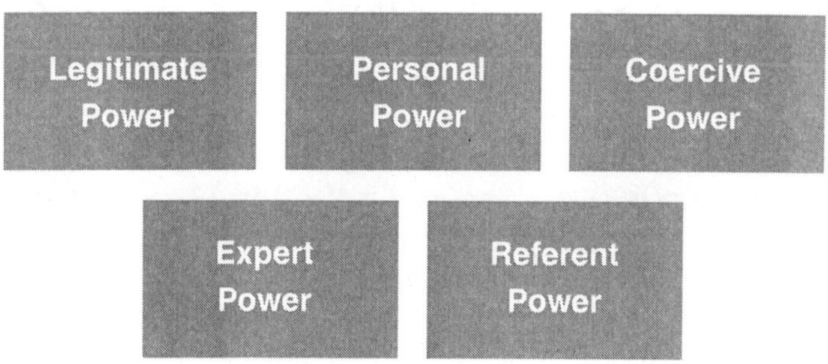

Legitimate Power is where a person in a higher position has control over people in a lower position in an organisation.

If you have this power, it's essential that you understand that this power was given to you (and can be taken away), so don't abuse it. If a women rises to the position of Chief executive officer (CEO) and her employees believe she deserves this position, they will respond favourably when she exercises her legitimate power. On the other hand, if a women rises to the position of Chief executive officer (CEO), but people don't believe that she deserves this power, it will be a bad move for the company as a whole.

Coercive Power is where a person leads threats and force. It is unlikely to win respect and loyalty from employees for long.

There is not a time of day when you should use it, Ultimately, you can't build credibility with coercive influence — you can think of it like bullying in the workplace.

Expert Power is the perception that one possesses superior skills or knowledge.

If a women holds an MBA and a PhD in statistical analysis, her colleagues and reports are more inclined to accede to her expertise.

In order to keep their status and influence, however, experts need to continue learning and improving.

Informational Power is where a person possesses needed or wanted information. This is a short-term power that doesn't necessarily influence or build credibility.

For example, a project manager may have all the information for a specific project, and that will give her informational power. But it's hard for a person to keep this power for long, and eventually this information will be released. This should not be a long-term strategy.

Reward Power is where a person motivates others by offering raises, promotions, and awards.

When you start talking financial livelihood, power takes on a whole new meaning. For example, both women and men hold a certain amount of reward power if they administer performance reviews that determine raises and bonuses for their people.

Connection Power is where a person attains influence by gaining favour or simply acquaintance with a powerful person. This power is all about networking.

If I have a connection with someone that you want to get to, that's going to give me power. That's politics in a way, People employing this power build important coalitions with others... Womens natural ability to forge such connections with individuals and assemble them into coalitions gives her strong connection power.

Referent Power is the ability to convey a sense of personal acceptance or approval. It is held by people with charisma, integrity, and other positive qualities. It is the most valuable type of power.

People with high referent power can highly influence anyone who admires and respects them.

Power struggles happen

When there is a clearly identified power struggle it is best to take it head on and not try to sweep it under the carpet. Limits have to be set and it has to be ensured that human dignity is maintained at all costs. Izzat or respect is a very important Eastern Concept the dignity of a person should not be lost that would do irreparable damage to the company hence communication also becomes very important Communication has two forms reasoned, rational based on facts and figures. Conversely, Highly charged and emotional, largely Irrational, rooted in primordial biases and prejudices, caste, class and gender. When these three primordial biases intertwine all rationality is lost. Communication is the key to resolution of a power struggle which by its very nature is a zero sum game. Primitive communication should never be allowed to override rationality.

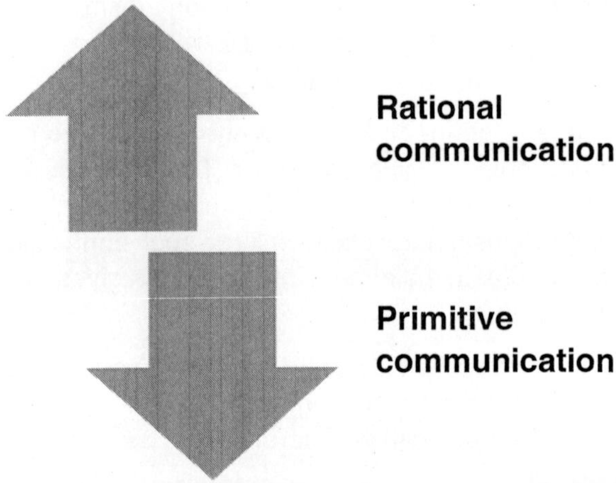

The primitive communication arises when the other party grows defensive. It focusses on territory, body language and voice inflection. Rational Communication focusses on words and their logical context. What is a power struggle let us put it simply: (1) Any situation where a group of people e.g. a Union

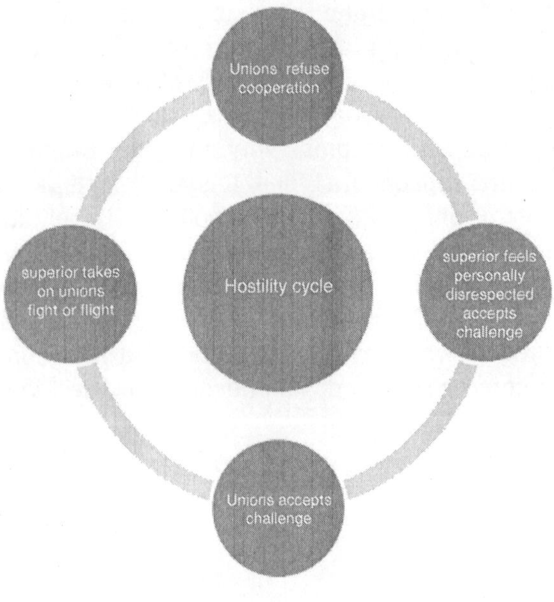

decides to take on the management and to not cooperate this can also be (2) bilateral a struggle for power between two individuals, subordinate superior (3) two peers, One decides not to cooperate and the other continues to engage. In any struggle there is a certain cycle let us call it the hostility cycle which reaches a point of irreconcilable inflection when fight or flight is the only possible resolution.

The Employer attempts to engage and the employee to deflect stout in rejection of any compromise solution. Women outperform men in their ability to be resolute and to resolve conflict situations at work. At the root of the power struggle is the need for control, power, recognition, respect and belonging it arises due to the dysfunctionality and largeness and general anonymity of large organisations. Women can better defuse tensions and empathetically engage with employees to foster a sense of loyalty. The four most common types of power struggles to avoid are personalised power struggles here one ends up trying to defend your authority, or credibility, reacting to personal button pushing. Issuing unenforceable consequences and getting sidetracked by irrelevant issues. It is always best and women are better at enforcing clear objective limits and then enforcing the consequences. The clear limits become choices.

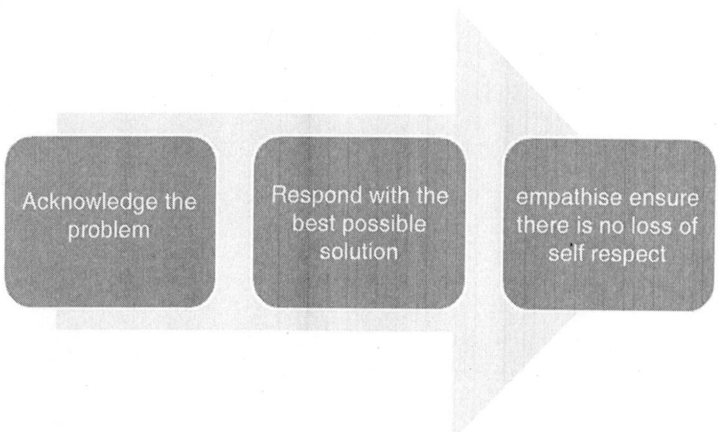

Women are thus better at processes of listening prevention of conflict intervention in conflict and in defusing the situation of conflict. This is what is meant by the appropriate and judicious exercise of power.

Chapter 8

Way Forward Learning to Fly

Women, on Corporate Boards should take the responsibilities that devolve upon them by virtue of the position they occupy seriously. As discussed in the previous pages, women have some natural skills, as people skills that they can hone to advantage. Other skills are to be acquired and built upon. On Board positions, judgement calls have to be taken. Part of judgement is hard to define and harder still to acquire. Some parts of good judgement or discernment are innate/ instinctive and have a lot to do with corporate governance the inbuilt code of ethics a balanced character and an understanding of other people. There is always scope for improvement in taking a judgement call rather than merely relying on a gut feeling women should base our judgement on data and information. Financial records and hard data should form the basis for effective decision-making. Judgement dictates the choice of strategy. This choice must suit the particular context the contingency the situation that the firm is faced with and should be able to meet the demands of the particular case. As effective leaders women should be able to look ahead, anticipate what is coming and move quickly and decisively to adjust to the new reality. Optimism goes a long way in keeping people motivated and charged up. This should not be misplaced megalomaniacal heroism it should also not be messianic and delusional. The psychology in good times is naturally, optimistic, aggressive and oriented towards increasing profits and revenue growth. In good times the rising tide lifts all boats, bad times are the true test of the woman leader's mettle. Those who were earlier energised should not be overwhelmed by events to the extent that they are unable to respond correctly or adequately to the demands of the changed circumstances. Under all circumstances, good or bad, triumph or disaster women as leaders need to keep a cool head and to be dispassionate and completely objective. An independent and careful evaluation of the facts is required at all times. Looking at things from a fresh perspective can reveal new realms of advantage and opportunity as well as weakness and threat. There is also a need to prioritise their allocation of time better. There are always only twenty four hours to the day. There has to be greater delegation as members on the Board Women should not try to involve themselves with every single operational nitty gritty of the day-to-day functioning of the company. To do this would be an extravagance in terms of time and would be to court disaster. They should concern themselves broadly with active engagement in the processes of macro prudential policy formulation.

WOMEN NEED TO LEARN TO HANDLE STRESS BETTER

Stress as External Force

The external force approach to the phenomenon of stress focuses on the circumstances which people experience as stressful. Stress is considered an independent variable, more or less beyond the control of the individual. According to Psychologists the stressful stimuli are:

- Speed-up information processing
- Noxious environmental stimuli
- Perceived threat
- Disrupted psychological function
- Isolation and confinement

- Blocking
- Group pressures and
- Frustrations

Psychological Function

Stress is considered as a response to a situation which demands that the individual adapt to a change physically or psychologically.

The theory of 'General Adaptation Syndrome' states that when an organism is confronted with a threat the general physiological response occurs in three stages:

Alarm Reaction: The first stage includes an initial 'shock phase' in which resistance is lowered, and a 'counter-shock phase' in which defensive mechanisms become active.

Alarm Reaction is characterised by autonomous excitability; adrenalin discharge; increased heart rate; muscle tone, and blood content; and gastro-intestinal ulceration. Depending on the nature and intensity of threat and the conditions of the organism, the periods of resistance vary and the severity of symptoms may differ from a mild invigoration to disease of adaption.

Stage of Resistance: Maximum adaptation occurs during this stage. The bodily signs characteristic of the alarm reaction disappear. Resistance increase to levels above normal. If the stressor persists, or the defensive reaction proves ineffective, the organism deteriorates to the next stage.

State of Exhaustion: Adaptation energy is exhausted, signs of alarm reaction reappear, and resistance level begins to decline irreversibly. The organism collapse.

A diagrammatic view of these stages is shown in figure I.

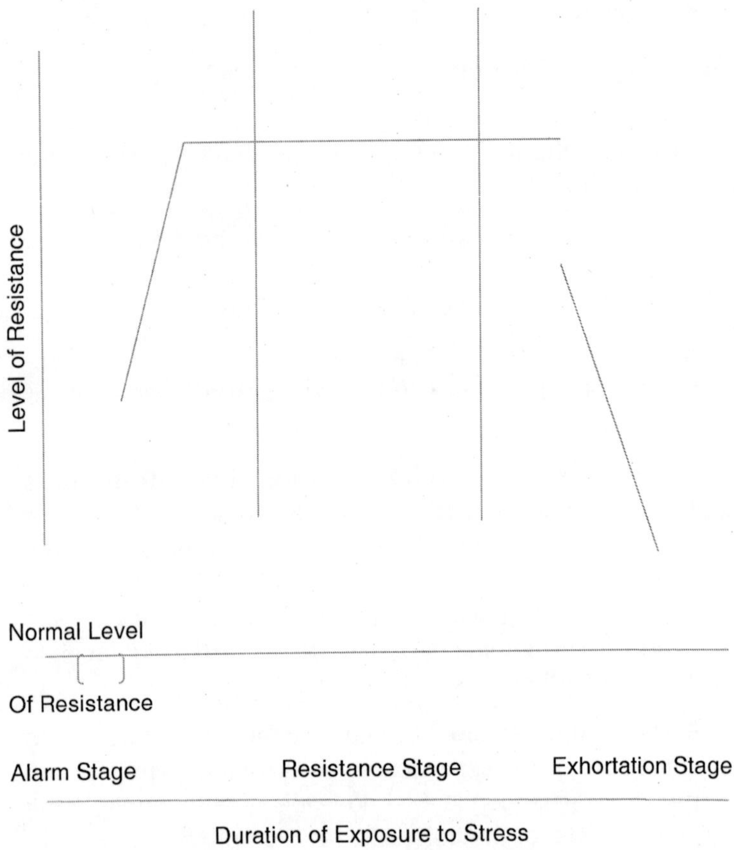

Figure I: General Adaptation Syndrome

One of the major shortcomings of this theory is that the related research was carried out on infra-human subjects, where the stressors are usually physical or environmental and this is not always the case in relation to human organisms.

Interactive Approach: According to this approach, stress is looked upon as an interactional outcome of the external demand and internal resources. McGrath explains, There is a potential for stress when an environmental situation is perceived as presenting the demand which threatens to exceed the person's capacities and resources for meeting it, under condition where he has expected a substantial differential in the rewards and costs from meeting the demand versus not meeting it.

Comprehensive Approach: This approach views stress not only in interactive terms but also as an individual phenomenon peculiar to the individual and his environment. It is seen as the situational outcome.

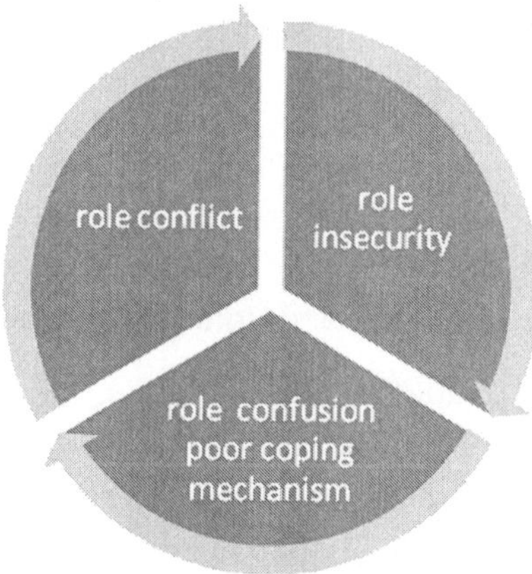

Role conflicts are some of the common dilemmas women confront. These lead to a build up of stress and which completely drain their energies. They also suffer from various insecurities as is evident from some of the common statements frequently heard and reiterated in the taxonomy given below:

1. Role conflict: My role tends to interfere with my family life.
2. I am not able to satisfy the conflicting demands of various people over me.
3. I have to do things in my role that are against my better judgement.

4. I am afraid I am not capable I do not know enough.
5. I am not learning enough in my present role for taking up higher responsibility.
6. My role has recently been reduced in importance.
7. My workload is too heavy.
8. Other role occupants do not give enough attention and time to my role.
9. I do not have adequate knowledge to handle the responsibilities in my role.
10. I am not clear on the scope and responsibilities of my role (job).
11. I do not get information needed to carry out responsibilities assigned to me.
12. I am not able to cope with all the conflicting and pressing demands being made on me.

Motivation and Morale

Important Components and determinants of morale are

(1) Feeling of Togetherness.
(2) Achievement of Goal.
(3) Expectation of success in the achievement of goals.
(4) She also matters whatever may be the job assigned to her.
(5) Supportive and stimulative leadership.
(6) All these determinants of morale are equivalent to that of job satisfaction which is a precursor of morale. However, the two differ as the term job satisfaction is used for individuals and morale for groups.

An enlightened management should be conscious of the need for assessing the morale of its employees by opinion pool or attitude survey from time to time. Low morale can be caused by factors beyond the control of the organisation. However, workers morale can be boosted up by (a) better methods of working in which workers or their representatives may have a bigger say, (b) utilisation of incentive schemes with the widest possible coverage and (c) consultative and participative style of management.

What Demotivates or Demoralises the Employees?

There are some management practices which affect the morale and motivation or willingness of workmen to give their best or work in the desired manner. Some of these practices are:

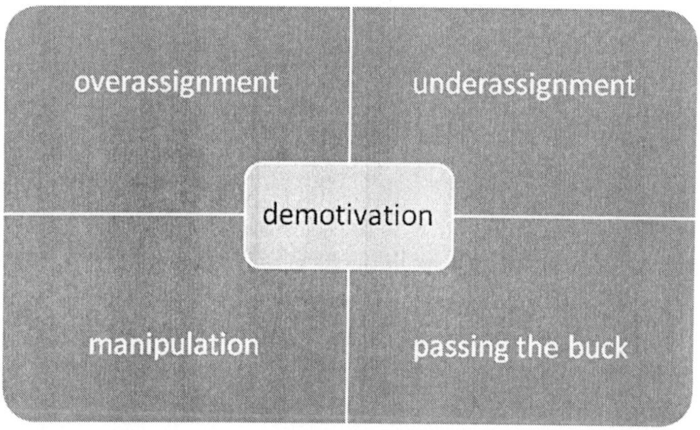

(a) **Under assignment**: If a skilled man is assigned an unskilled or routine job, it may cause frustration or job dissatisfaction and thus demotivation.

(b) **Over assignment**: If a good worker is overloaded to the point where he feels being exploited, this may make him lose interest in work. In big organisations, it is rather a common practice to pick up good workers as others cannot be trusted or depended upon.

(c) **Buckmastership**: An expression coined by Pakinson can also be a demotivator. Superiors or leaders avoiding hard work themselves and passing on the same to their subordinates, and hence finding fault with them is a common management practice which may erode employee motivation.

(d) **Coercive** types of control or supervision which may give a worker a feeling that he is not being trusted may also demotivate him or erode his interest in the work. Some control no doubt is essential but if it is too coercive resulting in frequent warnings or punishments, or withdrawal of facilities to chasten the employee, morale and motivation of the employee may go down.

(e) **Manipulative** behaviour of the management which may take the form of divide and rule policy or tactics, making promises which are not fulfilled, encouraging groupism and appealing to the patriotic sense in times of national crisis, may also have demotivating effect. When employees perceive such behaviour, they naturally cease to work and lose interest in the same.

Job Enrichment and Job Enlargement

Both these changes involve redesigning of the job and have the objective of humanising work by introducing more variety in work, increasing responsibilities, and making work more interesting, challenging and motivating. Job enlargement implies additions of more functions and increasing the variety of the task. But the additional responsibilities involved are of a horizontal nature. Job enrichment implies an improvement in the quality and variety of work and the additional responsibilities are of a critical nature encompassing self-control. Again the job enlargement merely makes a job structurally bigger, while job enrichment provides the opportunity for the employees' psychological growth. The job enrichment approach to job designing is therefore more often recommended by the behaviourists.

Characteristics underlying Job Enrichment

According to Hackman and Oldham, the following are the important job characteristics underlying job enrichment.

(a) **Skill Variety**: This provides opportunities for women employees to perform a wide range of operations of their work and use a wide variety of equipment and procedures.

(b) **Task Identity**: This allows women employees to do an entire or whole piece of work so that employees can clearly identify the result of their effort.

(c) **Task Significance**: This makes women employees feel that the job has a substantial impact on others. The impact can be on others in the organisation as when the worker performs a key step in the work process, or it may be on others outside the organisation, as when the worker helps to make a life saving instrument.

(d) **Autonomy**: This makes employees feel that the work is their own and they are responsible for whatever success or failure ensuing from their work. Autonomy measures the extent to which employees have a say in scheduling their work, selecting the equipment they will use, and deciding on procedure to be followed. The autonomy is created through a process of vertical loading that is, the worker is given self-management rights in multiple areas.

(e) **Feedback**: The worker must receive useful and believable information regarding the job performance. Feedback may come from the job itself or from the supervisor or from other persons.

Thus, women have contributed significantly to India's economic growth and progress and have the potential to make even greater contributions. The country should harness the talents and energies of its population and get at 100 per cent.

Confident in the capability of women's leadership will lead the century to emerge in the for front of the comity of nations us a economics Super power. A bold new emerging India must harness energy's of all it population.

Today women leadership is an idea whose times has come.

Index

D

E

F

G

H